Mrs Earle's Pot-Pourri

Mrs Earle's Pot-Pourri

Anne Jones

Illustrated by Prue Theobalds

British Broadcasting Corporation

To Lieutenant-Colonel and Mrs Charles Earle

For you there's rosemary and rue;
These keep seeming and savour all the winter long.
Grace and remembrance be to you both
And welcome to our shearing.

(*The Winter's Tale*, Act 4, Scene 4)

The Radio 4 feature *Mrs Earle's Surrey Garden* was first broadcast in 1981 and repeated in 1982. It was written and narrated by Anne Jones and produced by Pamela Howe.

Published by the
British Broadcasting Corporation
35 Marylebone High Street
London W1M 4AA
ISBN 0 563 20089 8
First published 1982

Contents

My grateful thanks are due to:
Lieutenant-Colonel Charles Earle for his interest
and help, particularly for the loan of his
photograph album, miniature and Mrs Earle's
parasol shown on the jacket, and for access to
private family papers.
Canon Dennis C. Moore of St Mary's Church,
Watford, for permission to use the extract quoted
on page 11, and my admiration for a filing system
which enabled him to produce, without a
moment's pause, copies of his church's magazines
of more than a hundred years earlier.
Messrs. Suttons Seeds Ltd and Thompson and
Morgan Ltd for allowing me to examine catalogues
from their archives.
Lastly, very special gratitude to Sheila Elkin, the
editor, Veronica Loveless, the designer, and Prue
Theobalds, the illustrator, for their
unflagging interest.

Anne Jones

The
Patient Gleaner

In the late summer of 1896, Maria Theresa Earle, resident of the suburb of Cobham in the County of Surrey, parcelled up and posted off to a firm of London publishers, the handwritten manuscript of a book that was to 'startle the critics', make 'Mrs Earle' into a household name, and the publishers, Smith, Elder & Company, richer by more than £30,000.

Neither they – nor she – can have dreamt that just one more book by just one more Victorian lady would shortly be in such popular demand that eleven more editions were to be rushed into the shops in its first year; there were twenty-eight eventually, and several translations. On publication day, with the cream of London's fashionable society crowding into Hatchards' demanding copies of 'Theresa's book', a salesman was heard to remark, a trifle waspishly, that he didn't call it a literary success at all – merely a social one. But of course it was more than that. One shop full of the book-buying beau-monde could hardly have made 'Pot-pourri from a Surrey Garden' into the national and international best-seller it became; nor the two following, 'More Pot-pourri from a Surrey Garden' and 'A Third Pot-pourri'. Although exactly where lay – and still lies – their particular charm, is not easy to define.

The titles, if repetitive, do have a certain evocative allure – particularly for a nation of gardeners, few of whom, in 1896, actually had gardens; or so the publishers thought. It was

7

they who insisted on keeping the 'pot-pourri' element in the second and third titles, even though Theresa was by now thoroughly disenchanted with the word. 'So sad,' she wrote, 'to have to repeat that most un-English word in that most tiresome title.'

In any case, she had never expected to write more than one book; but then, neither had she expected the overwhelming public response to her first. Letters had been arriving by the sackful; complimentary, in most cases, but there had been the odd note of disapproval. Wouldn't another book be a wonderful opportunity to reply to her critics?

Not many writers would be able to resist such a temptation. Indeed, not many writers would even be offered it. But by now, Smith, Elder must have known they were on to a winner, and let her get away with fourteen pages of retort, retaliation and general tit-for-tat. Mrs Earle, it transpired, could give back every bit as good as she got.

'I have been *overwhelmed*,' she wrote, tongue firmly in cheek, 'with suggestions about the future and what I should and should not do. Some have said – and these are the most earnest in their heart-felt appeals – that I should rest on my laurels and write no more. I agree with this view . . . up to the point of not acting upon it.'

She reported, with undisguised glee, that her recipes had caused 'panic in some minds and indignation in others', and dismissed a complaint about her uncertain grammar as 'a bit of pedantic purism.' But, clearly, she was herself faintly mystified by her own success, agreeing disarmingly with some critics, and having 'considerable sympathy' with one who said, as the book went soaring into its eighth edition, that he 'couldn't conceive why, as there was nothing to it'. She couldn't conceive why, either. 'A curious vein of flattery that ran through dozens of the letters was expressive of the writers' regret that they had not written "Pot-pourris" of their own' she observed – 'proving the general truth of how easy everything is, if we only take the trouble to do it.'

Mrs Earle had indeed found writing a great trouble. Many

1 *Family group at Government House, Isle of Man. Theresa and Charles, recently engaged, on extreme left, next Henry Loch, Governor, Theresa's sister Elizabeth Loch and brother Ernest. Cousin Henry Trotter and Elizabeth's twin sister Edith, sit at the feet of the Hon. Mrs Elizabeth Villiers.*

2 *The conservatory at Woodlands.*

3 *Family (Sidney, centre back, Maxwell on his left, Lionel front) and friends at Woodlands about 1898. Mrs Earle often attempted match-making, but with little success. 'The young girls I liked were speedily called "Mother's friends"' wrote Maxwell.*

4 *Garden at Woodlands, from the terrace.*

5 *The Woodlands sundial, part of the balustrade from the old Kew bridge, demolished 1889. 'I do not think a sundial is affected . . . at any rate, not very . . .' wrote Theresa.*

6 *Mrs Earle at Woodlands, aged 83.*

years later, she explained: 'I have often been asked how I, who had never written, came to write the first "Pot-pourri" in my old age. It came about in this way. My foreign friend, Madame de Grunelius, came to stay with us in our new London house in Cadogan Gardens, and as she was furnishing a country house near Frankfort, I began telling her all I knew both as regards furnishing and gardening. She naturally got rather bewildered and said "Oh, I shall never remember all this; if you would write it down, I should be so grateful". So I began to write, and I found it a good deal of trouble as I was nursing my dear niece Constance Lytton at the top of the house through an attack of measles at the time. But we both thought – if all this is to be so useful to Madame de Grunelius, why not to others? And in this way the book took shape. But for my niece and her help it would never have been finished, and but for her would probably have been consigned to the flames. In writing the book, under the impression that it would be an absolute failure, I used to console myself by saying "Well, if it helps ten people just a little, that makes it worth while". My hope and wish was that my reader would take me by the hand, for I do not reap and I do not sow. I am merely, like so many other women of the past and present, a patient gleaner in the fields of knowledge, and absolutely dependent on human sympathy in order to do anything at all'.

She was too modest. Mrs Earle – Theresa, Teasie, Aunt T., Teasums, Radical T – sometimes just T – was already firmly established in her own circle as an authority and dispenser of much sound advice on every conceivable subject, every possible problem. By contemporary standards she was widely-travelled, experienced, well-read, progressive, sensible – above all, *practical*; that most esteemed Victorian virtue. What could be more praiseworthy, then – was it not even her Christian duty – to put all this wise counsel at the disposal of others less competent? Of course . . . put like that . . .

Only one member of the family doggedly refused to join in the chorus urging Theresa to take up her pen – that was her husband, Charles. Grievously alarmed by the entire project, he was driven, in despair, to offer her £100 if only she would abandon the idea. But it was too late by then; once into her literary stride, Theresa was unstoppable and, in the event, when Charles read the finished product he 'smiled, and was pleased – an immense joy to me'. Safely home and dry, she was able to add virtuously '. . . for I was never happy under his disapproval'.

Perhaps unknown to Charles, however, Theresa had burst into print many years before – 'under the influence' as she explained 'of an adoring curate, who extracted from me two little articles about the Prince of Wales's marriage, and they appeared in the Watford parish magazines for March and April, 1863'. The extraction must have been fairly painless, as this was a subject close to Theresa's heart – marriage, in particular early marriage. 'I am an old woman now' she reflected, 'and have lived through many experiences with large family connexions on both sides, and am certain that I have never seen any one who would have suited me better or as well as my own husband; but he and I differed on many points, and he was especially against early marriage, above all for men; but I still believe that on the whole to marry before thirty is the best for both. A man who has been a good husband for many years to the girl of his choice is not likely to sow many wild oats as he gets older – or at any rate they would not be very bad wild oats; none that his wife in her matronly wisdom would not be able to ignore or forgive . . .'

As a feature written by a non-professional and inexperienced journalist, Theresa's pre-wedding article repays re-reading.

'It is the Prince himself who has fixed upon the Princess Alexandra, and his choice is approved of by all; for she is one of the fairest of European Princesses; and all, without exception, who have known her from childhood, or only now at this time of her girlish triumph, speak of her character and disposition in the highest terms of approbation . . .

'We sympathise warmly with him in his happiness, and

believe that if his young heart hopefully and trustfully
for the future, it is from right motives, and a belief that the
solemn step he is about to take, is for his country's good as
well as his own.

'The right loyal feelings of old England run as strong and
high as ever – and every newspaper teems with the coming
event, every county, town and hamlet is striving to make the
festal day one of loving congratulations and local rejoicings.
London is preparing to give the Danish Princess, about to become an English woman, as warm a welcome as ever met
King or Queen, or conquering hero. If we fail a little in the
taste of our decorations, or our streets are not lined with
proud palaces decked with glowing colours and costly
draperies; we shall nevertheless give her such a welcome as
none but Englishmen can give, and the one hearty British
cheer (*one* though from a million voices) that will greet her
during the seven miles transit across London, will be remembered throughout her life, though it be long or though it be
chequered (for who can tell the clouds that may arise to over-
shadow the brightest morning?) and she will ever look back
gratefully to that day – the first she spent amongst a people
henceforth to be her own'.

Stirring stuff. But it was Theresa's straight reportage of
the event itself that must have given the pre-radio, pre-TV
parishioners of Watford as true a picture of a royal wedding
as they could have hoped for.

'The day broke in London on a dense cold fog, and
brought the wish to thousands of hearts on that Tuesday
morning that the gloom might be only spread over London,
and the sky be clear and the sun bright above the towers of
old Windsor. And so it was. Those who were especially invited to the wedding by the Queen were conveyed to Windsor
by a special train, a little before 10 o'clock; those who only
had tickets for the nave of St George's chapel, had to go
earlier, for by eleven all were to be in their places, and the
doors closed. It was not till a few minutes before twelve that
the first procession was to pass through into the chapel,
which is screened off from the nave, so that none but those
actually inside could see the interior of the sacred edifice.

That hour of waiting seemed long to none, for there was much to look at. A continual passing to and fro of high officers of state, Archbishops and Bishops, Knights in flowing robes, hoary-headed Statesmen, and fair women, in all the pride of their youth and beauty; much to interest, much to amuse. Later came the Bridesmaids on their way to the room in which they were to await their Royal mistress, all dressed in cloudy white, with wreaths and bouquets of blush roses, heather and shamrock leaves, emblematical of course of the three kingdoms over which we earnestly hope the young Prince will some day be called to reign. At last there was an almost solemn stillness; all were in their places, all were ready. Then came the sound of cheering in the distance, and the subdued tones of the National Anthem, and all knew the first procession was on its way; on they came, a goodly train, the Royal Family of England, ushered in by drums and trumpets and all the pomp and pageantry of the throne. First came the Duchess of Cambridge and the Princess Mary, whose handsome face and noble bearing never fails to attract universal admiration. Then followed all the Royal Children – the Princess Alice leaning on her young husband's arm, and the Princess Royal leading her almost infant son. On reaching the end of the chapel, before they took the places allotted to them, each one made a low and reverential obeisance to England's Queen; for there she stood, that widowed Queen, clearly seen by all, as they gazed up into the Royal pew, which is a recess, high up in the left-hand wall of the chapel. Almost alone she stood, attended only by three ladies, widows like herself, in her simple weeds, the blue ribbon of the garter being her only distinguishing ornament, a heart-stirring contrast to all the brightness and splendour beneath her. The outward homage paid the Royal Mother by her Children, was one of the most touching sights of all that day.

'Next in order came the procession of the Bridegroom; he wore the robes of a knight of the garter, and as he passed he bowed a grave but gracious acknowledgment to those on the right hand and on the left, who bent their head and knee. He was supported on one side by his brother-in-law the Prince of Prussia, and on the other by his uncle, the Duke of Saxe

Coburg and Gotha. Allowing time for all the long train of Equerries and attendants which formed the Prince's procession, it was a quarter past twelve ere the cheers once more resounded outside, and all whispered with breathless interest "the Bride! She comes!" And all eyes were fixed on that young girl of nineteen; she walked calmly and slowly, and the only trace to be seen of the agitation it was but natural she should feel was a slight palor which overspread her handsome features, and the steadiness with which she kept her eyes fixed on the ground – never for one moment glancing upwards, or to the right or left. Her long bridal train, richly trimmed with lace and orange flower, was borne by eight young Bridesmaids, unmarried daughters of Dukes and Earls. As the Bride entered the choir, Handel's March from "Joseph" was played, and on her taking her seat, a chorale sung, composed by the late Prince Consort. The light shone palely through the memorial window above the altar, which had just been placed there in *his* name, and all thought solemnly and sadly of him, of Albert "The Good", whose empty place none could fill! The service was then performed by the Archbishop of Canterbury; and at the moment when the Princess Alexandra became Princess of Wales, the guns, fired in the long walk of Windsor Park, announced the joyful intelligence far and near. The sun burst forth with brilliant splendour, and a silent prayer for the happiness of the Prince and Princess rose up from the hearts of all present.'

*   *   *

Theresa didn't sign her name to either of these articles. When, a year or two earlier, she had thought about writing a book on art for amateurs she had abandoned the idea, being 'nervous' she said 'of seeing myself in print'. It was thirty-four years before she was able sufficiently to conquer her nerves and publish the first 'Pot-pourri' – 'by Mrs C. W. Earle'.

Even then, Theresa could so easily have written her book, had it published, only to watch it sink without trace, had it not been for the unexpected late flowering of that rare talent, honed by a lifetime of non-stop letter-writing, for transferring her individual, quirky charm, irresistibly on to the printed page.

Unaware of any such gift, she began cautiously, warning her readers not to expect too much. . . . 'I am not going to write a gardening book, or a cookery book, or a book on furnishing or education. Plenty of these have been published already', she wrote – and proceeded to write a book about gardening, cookery, furnishing and education. However, she went on: 'I merely wish to talk to you, on paper, about several subjects as they occur to me, and if such desultory notes prove to be of use to you or others, so much the better.'

Put another way – either take me or leave me alone. And, in the case of the latter, adding dolefully: 'Just now it seems as if everybody wrote books which nobody reads. That is probably what I am doing myself.'

What she was doing – in a brilliant flash of beginner's luck – was seizing her readers by the collar and challenging them to keep right on reading.

*   *   *

Commercial success, as best-selling author or anything else, was the least likely gift the most feminist of fairy godmothers would have thought of wishing for the baby Theresa Villiers. Her mother was the Hon. Elizabeth (née Liddell), ninth child of the first Baron Ravensworth; her father, the Hon. Edward, great-grandson of the second Earl of Jersey; blue-blooded aristocrats, both.

In retrospect, Theresa could view her parents objectively and sometimes critically. Both seem to have been mildly but congenitally depressive; shy, not over-endowed with optimism, permanently below par in health and spirits – Elizabeth in particular being in 'a constant state of repentance and self-reproach'. Not a condition conducive to excessive *joie de vivre*, her daughter felt.

But – Elizabeth was beautiful and Edward handsome and

despite – even, perhaps, because of – their shared low spirits, they were utterly content with each other; two personalities, fragile and uncertain when apart, complemented each other in marriage and grew strong. Edward was even able to crack the conjugal whip when he felt it called for. An apologetic little note from Elizabeth followed one domestic rift: 'Dearest Edward, I think I'm wrong and I'm sure I am unhappy. Pray forgive me and I will strive with all my might and at all costs to satisfy you on this point as on every other – and be down earlier of a morning. Your Elizabeth.'

Certainly they produced notable issue. After Theresa in 1836 came Ernest in 1838, and in 1841, the famous Villiers twins, who were to become renowned for their beauty and charm, Elizabeth, later Lady Loch, and Edith, later Lady Lytton.

But the happy marriage was not to last for long. Just eight years after their wedding, Edward died of consumption, aged thirty-seven. Theresa was seven years old, Ernest five and the twins, two.

Immediately, Elizabeth slipped into a role which might have been designed for her; describing herself as 'the poor pale widow', for the rest of her long life she performed this part to perfection. Even though, two days after Edward's death, she was writing to her father: 'I expect to have rather better than £1,000 a year, and no incumbrances whatever', she presented herself thereafter as being permanently on the brink of penury – a predilection enthusiastically shared by her eldest daughter. 'Then, nearly all the charming, attractive people one knew were somewhat morbid and sentimental', Theresa wrote, thirty years later; and in an age that deliberately cultivated 'a delightful melancholy', the pensive young widow and her fatherless children must have presented an appealing picture. But, surrounded as they were by kind and wealthy friends and relatives, the pinch of poverty can't ever have been too painful. The little family always contrived to live in houses that were beautiful, if borrowed, with a devoted, if small, staff. All the springs and summers of Theresa's childhood were spent at Grove Mill House, the dower house of The Grove, Watford, estate of her uncle, the fourth Earl of Clarendon; it is the old-fashioned garden of this house of which she writes so evocatively in the Pot-pourri books. Travelling on the continent, they stayed at the slightly less fashionable places – but they were, nevertheless, of the aristocracy, recognised as such, and behaved accordingly. They travelled, they socialised. Theresa was presented at Court. She was invited to become one of Queen Victoria's Maids of Honour, although, in a spasm of what she later felt may have been somewhat confused reasoning, refused. But it was these years as the allegedly 'poor relation' that Theresa believed equipped her for what she expected – even, she claimed, hoped – to be her destined role in life – that of a poor man's wife.

That she was likely to be anyone's wife at all was highly doubtful for some time. She had met Captain Charles Earle in Florence in 1857, then again later in London, when he had revealed 'with great frankness . . . his feelings for me', which feelings were not reciprocated for the best possible reason. Theresa was in love with someone else. So Charles went off to India with his regiment, and there remained for seven years. Theresa meantime remained faithful to her first love. But not even the most romantically-inclined Victorian maiden could be expected to languish for ever. With the return of Captain Charles imminent, her mother became suddenly businesslike, insisting that Theresa consider and decide what she intended doing about the two men in her life. Theresa considered, and decided. Charles came home, proposed again and, this time, was accepted. Family and friends were delighted – most of them, said Theresa, having quite given her up by this time; she was twenty-seven.

'What pleased me was that they all seemed to acknowledge that I was fit to be a poor man's wife, which I sincerely felt to be my one real vocation.'

But even for Theresa, with her penchant for poverty, there were limits. Her own legacy of £6,000 was still in trust;

Charles was out of the army and out of a job; marriage seemed a remote prospect. Then, once again, the family came to the rescue. 'Kind uncle Clarendon' offered an allowance of £100; this tipped the scales, and Theresa and Charles were married on 14 April 1864, at St Paul's, Knightsbridge.

*   *   *

So at last, Theresa was a – comparatively – poor man's wife; which she seemed to enjoy rather more than Charles enjoyed being a – comparatively – poor man. He was often ill, she nursing him back to health with relentless efficiency. They moved house a lot. Charles's various excursions into commerce were never entirely successful. For fifteen years they rarely went out into society, and, during these quiet years, their three sons were born (Sydney in 1865, Lionel in 1866 and, in 1871, Maxwell) and Theresa began forming the strong opinions and acquiring the expertise that she was later to write about.

But her days as poor man's wife were numbered. Within the space of two years, two of Charles's brothers died, naming him their heir; two years later again saw the death of his father. Suddenly they were not merely more comfortably off; they were extremely rich.

From now on, the Earles' lives followed the conventional Victorian upper-class pattern. Their sons were expensively educated; they socialised, travelled, entertained in London and at their country house in Cobham, 'Woodlands' – from which, years later, Theresa was to be launched on her literary career.

> 'We decided to get some small country place where we were to live half the year, the other half in London. People with fixed ideas of what they want know the almost impossibility of finding it. We were no exception to this rule, and in despair we fixed at last on a house and garden far below our ideals, but my husband would not build, preferring, as he said, the faults of others to those of his own making. Improv-

ing the place was an amusement to both of us, and he delighted in having horses in the stables he had built, which were a cross between a Burne-Jones studio and a Dutch house. The sons always declared that the two Scotch firs at the end of the garden really, as far as my opinion went, decided the purchase. I found the difficulty of conquering the Bagshot sand a most useful exercise for a gardener. During the first two years, from my ignorance and inexperience of anything but the heavy soil of Hertfordshire, everything I planted died. When we first came here, the place, the village and the surroundings, were quite extraordinarily countrified, rural and quiet, considering how near to London it was. We were three and a half miles from a station before the new Guildford line was opened.' But . . . 'time runs quickly on, and for more than six years we continued to lead much the same life – London in the winter, Woodlands in the summer. As I got to know more, my keenness about gardening increased, and I used to come down three times every winter to look after the garden, and the gardener and his wife looked after me. The dear sons grew into men, always coming and going, my four men were always about me, and I had the ever-living interest in all their lives.'

She was supremely happy – and perhaps the high water-mark of Theresa's life was that Whit Sunday morning in 1897; surrounded by loving family and good friends, her first book on its way from the publishers; life must have seemed very good.

Two days later, Charles was dead, killed in a road accident five miles from home. 'That was the end,' Theresa wrote. 'Everything, afterwards, was different.'

But it wasn't the end. Two years later, Sydney, the eldest of those three dear sons was also dead, killed in action in South Africa. His youngest brother Maxwell, a Grenadier, fighting in the same battle, wrote in his diary: ' . . . as I was advancing, a riderless horse came through the line from the rear and galloped down towards me. It was Syd's horse.'

*   *   *

At the end of the third 'Pot-pourri', dedicated to the memory of her eldest son, Theresa published his last letters. 'It was he who encouraged me,' she wrote, 'when under the shadow of another sorrow, to write my second book, and it is indeed to his memory and with absolute confidence of his approval that I dedicate my third.

'I am in no sense a worthy mother of soldiers. I gave him very grudgingly to the army, and he knew quite well all it meant to me. I think he knew quite well, too, as we walked round the garden for the last time, that we should never meet again. I gave him to die for his country not willingly at all, and I publish these letters because it is a pleasure to myself to see them in print'. And she quoted Fuller Maitland's poem:

> Home now your comrades come again,
> But you come not.
> For them life's triumphs still remain
> You draw Death's lot.
>
> Oh, lying far from home away
> Feel not so far;
> For, though all come, my heart does stay
> There, where you are.

*   *   *

As we have seen, the six years during which the 'Pot-pourri' trilogy was written saw great changes in Theresa Earle's life and circumstances. In 1897 she was a happy, much-loved wife and mother of three splendid sons, a successful and popular hostess, moving in court, diplomatic and artistic circles. Six years later she was a widow and alone; one son was dead, the second living away from home, the third and youngest married and in the army.

But life went on. After a while she closed the house in Cadogan Gardens, but continued to visit in London and to travel about this country and on the continent. Her circle of friends never diminished and with one, Ethel Case, she wrote two more books, 'Pot-pourri Mixed by Two' and 'Gardening for the Ignorant'. In 1911, at the age of seventy-five, Theresa published her tour-de-force, the vast family history, 'Memoirs and Memories', dedicating it *To my grandchildren, Margaret and Evelyn Earle,* daughters of her youngest son, Maxwell. He, the only one of the Earle boys to father children of his own, had married his first cousin, Edith Loch; besides the two little girls, they had a son Charles, born in 1913, now Lieutenant-Colonel Earle, DSO, OBE, of Yeovil in Somerset.

Theresa's 'Woodlands' has gone now, her garden divided into smaller plots for smaller houses, but another 'Woodlands' is built on the site. Rhododendrons still line the drive and there are traces of the old walls.

There is, too, an unofficial memorial to Mrs Earle – perhaps the one she would most of all have preferred. Her second son, Lionel, inheritor of her abiding love for nature, plants and wild life, became, in 1912, Permanent Secretary to the then Ministry of Works (now the Department of the Environment) with particular responsibility for London's parks and gardens, a position he held for more than twenty years.

Although arranged month by month, the following extracts are taken from Mrs Earle's writings over several years. However, specific years are given only when their omission might cause confusion.

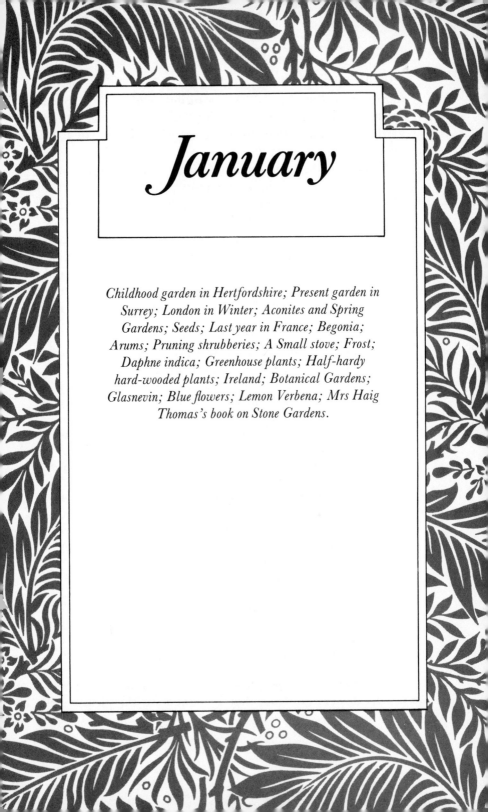

January

*Childhood garden in Hertfordshire; Present garden in
Surrey; London in Winter; Aconites and Spring
Gardens; Seeds; Last year in France; Begonia;
Arums; Pruning shrubberies; A Small stove; Frost;
Daphne indica; Greenhouse plants; Half-hardy
hard-wooded plants; Ireland; Botanical Gardens;
Glasnevin; Blue flowers; Lemon Verbena; Mrs Haig
Thomas's book on Stone Gardens.*

I shall begin by telling you that I was brought up for the most part in the country, in a beautiful, wild, old-fashioned garden. This garden had remained in the hands of an old gardener for more than thirty years, which carries us back nearly a century, to 1796.

Almost all that has remained in my mind of my young days in this garden is how wonderfully the old man kept the place. He succeeded in flowering many things, year after year, with no one to help him and with the frost in the valley to contend with in Spring. The spot was very sheltered, and that is one of the greatest of all secrets for plant cultivation. An ever-flowing mill-stream ran all round the garden and the hedges of China Roses, Sweetbriar, Honeysuckle and White Hawthorn tucked their toes into the soft mud, and throve year after year.

> This was the garden to Grove Mill House, the dower house on The Grove estate, the seat of the fourth Earl of Clarendon, Theresa's uncle, and where Theresa and her sisters and brother spent all the springs and summers of their youth.
>
> Grove Mill house is privately-owned now, and The Grove estate is the property of British Rail, used as their staff training college. Prior to this it has been a health farm, a gardening school, and a school for girls – also the headquarters of the National Institute of Nutrition and College of Dietetics. Under the jurisdiction of the Department of the Environment it is listed as a Grade II building and kept in excellent repair. When, in 1920, The Grove was put up for sale, *The Times* published a letter deploring the passing of 'one of the great political houses of the nineteenth century. In these degenerate days it may be necessary to call it The Grove, Watford, but, to our grandfathers, The Grove needed no suffixes. Thanks to its nearness to London, The Grove must have been one of the first houses where the practice of Saturday to Monday visiting (as the weekend habit was then called) was in force.' (from 'The Grove Story' by Dennis A. Lovett).

Like so many young people I see about me now, I cared only for the flowers growing, that I might have the pleasure of picking them. Mr Ruskin says that it is luxurious and pleasure-loving people who like them gathered. Gardening is, I think, essentially the amusement of the middle-aged and old. The lives of the young are, as a rule, too full to give the time and attention required.

In his book 'In a Gloucestershire Garden', Canon Henry Ellacombe ends with a warning to the clergy against gardening as being too interesting and too absorbing an occupation for them. I can thoroughly echo this sentiment as a warning to all young people. It can only be perfectly indulged in by the lonely and the old, or by those who do not mind neglecting their own duties and who say, bravely and honestly 'I am quite selfish and quite happy'.

Yet, owing to the vivid character of the impressions of youth, I was left with a memory that was very useful to me when I took up gardening later in life.

To this day I can smell the tall white double Rockets that throve so well in the damp garden and scented the evening air. They grew by the side of the glorious bunches of Oriental Poppies and the oncoming (*sic*) spikes of the feathery *Spiraea aruncus*. This garden had such peculiar charms for us because, though we hardly realised it, such gardens were already beginning to grow out of fashion, sacrificed to the new bedding-out system, which altered the whole gardening of Europe. I shall allude to this again.

She did, she did. See pages 50, 51, 92, 147.

The garden I have now is a small piece of flat ground surrounding an ordinary suburban house. Kitchen-garden, flower-garden, house and drive can scarcely cover more than two acres. The garden is surrounded by large forest trees, Spanish Chestnuts and Oaks, whose wicked roots walk into all the beds almost as fast as we can cut them off. The soil is dry, light and sandy and ill-adapted to garden purposes. We are only sixteen miles from London, and on unfavourable days, when the wind is in the blighting south-east, the afternoons are darkened by the smoke of the huge city.

People often envy me my house in London, and say 'What could you do in the Surrey garden in the winter?' But no true gardener would make this remark, as there is much to be done at all times and seasons. Half the interest of a garden is the constant exercise of the imagination. You are always living three, or indeed, six months hence. I believe that people entirely devoid of imagination never can be really good gardeners. To be content with the present, and not striving about the future, is fatal.

But it seems almost useless to describe my garden. Though I myself am so very fond of it, there is no reason anyone else should understand why I love it; and when I read the descriptions of the gardens that other people love, I wonder I can bear with it at all.

It is surrounded, as I said, with large forest trees and that most objectionable of conifers, a Wellingtonia, grows almost in the middle of the garden. I cannot cut it down, as this would deprive the lawn-tennis ground of the only shade it has. How I long to turn that lawn-tennis ground into a sunk Dutch garden, with its low red wall all round it! Yet I know I should miss them very much if I no longer heard the cries of the lawn-tennis game or the more recent click of the croquet-balls.

The first Aconite! Does any flower in summer give the same pleasure? I find that even in this dry soil the Aconites do much better under evergreens and at the edges of shrubs than in the borders, which are manured and mulched. The borders are too good for them, and they increase better if not disturbed. I mention this, as I was so stupidly long in finding it out myself. The more the uneducated gardening mind cares about a plant, the more it turns to manure and mulching; but in many cases it does more harm than good – notably with Aconites, Daffodils, Scillas, etc. What they all want is moisture and protection at the growing time. Drying ever so much in the summer does them good rather than harm, and they never do well in a bed that is hosed or

watered to suit other things. With the Aconites, our first out-
door friends, come a few Snowdrops. They have never been
planted here in any quantity, and have a tendency to diminish rather than increase; perhaps mice are especially fond of
them. I am more than ever determined to plant a large quantity next year; enough, if possible, for me and the mice too.

The blue-green blades of the Daffodils and Jonquils are
firmly and strongly pushing through the cold brown earth;
nothing in all the year gives such a sense of power and joy.
One is grateful, too, for our Surrey soil and climate – to live
where it never can rain too much and where these mild winters have a wonderful effect on plant life. The *Solanum jasmi-
noides* looks as fresh as in November, and as if he meant to
stand it out. We shall see.

I think the multiplicity of nurserymen, small and great,
and the gardeners' sympathy with the trade, have had much
to do with the fact that the sowing of seeds, except in the case
of annuals, has gone so out of fashion. No matter where I go,
it is not one garden in a hundred that has these permanent
small nurseries for seeds or even for cuttings, or a reserve
garden. And yet I am sure many of the best perennials cannot be grown at all in a light sandy soil unless they are grown
from seed on the spot, and a great many more are only to be
seen in real perfection if they are treated as annuals or bi-
ennials. The growing of seeds is work which an amateur
gardener can see to himself – or indeed, herself, and I am
sure gardening is the healthiest occupation in the world, as it
keeps one much out of doors. Instead of lolling indoors in
comfortable chairs, one moves about, and with the mind
fully occupied all the time.

I always order all the kitchen garden seeds during January. My method is this – the gardener marks Sutton's list,
and then brings it to me to alter or add to it any out-of-the-
way vegetables. It is most important to go through the catalogues and order seeds early in the month. This enables you

to get first choice, and you are then prepared for any kind of weather, and can sow early if desirable. However, it is a great mistake, when marking the nurseryman's seed list, to order those vegetables described as 'giant', 'large', 'perfection', etc. Such vegetables do *not* grow large – and they *do* grow tough and tasteless.

For all the flower seeds that are the result of careful cultivation, such as Sweet peas, Mignonette, Asters, Salpiglossis and so on, the great nurserymen cannot, of course, be surpassed in excellence. But for small people who grow a variety of flowers, they are very expensive, as they only sell large packets of seeds, have few things out of the common, and hardly any interesting perennials at all. I have said before, and shall continue to say that, for all uncommon seeds, there is one man without any rival as far as I know, and that is Mr Thompson of Ipswich. His catalogue alone is most descriptive and instructive. It is the only catalogue I know arranged simply and alphabetically with a column telling whether the plants are hardy or half-hardy, tender or perennial, greenhouse, stove, etc. It is also the only catalogue which gives the approximate height that the plant ought to reach when grown to perfection.

Mr William Thompson, founder of the firm of Thompson & Morgan, is still known as the Baker-Botanist. Born in 1803 over his family's bakery in Tavern Street, Ipswich, his early interest in photography led to the study of botany and then to the cultivation of the little garden at the rear of the shop. From these small beginnings developed three large nurseries, and the publication, in 1885, of the first catalogue.

1885 saw the introduction of more capital and a partner, Mr John Morgan – and the formation of the still-flourishing firm of Thompson & Morgan. It is now owned and operated by the brothers Keith and Bruce Sangster.

During our short stay in France last year, I saw several gardens but nothing at all interesting. As we drove through the villages I noticed specimens of a white variety of *Iberis gibral-*

tarica (Candytuft) grown in pots, carefully pruned and cared for, standing in the windows of the cottages. Managed in this way, it made a very charming Spring pot-plant. I have never seen it so treated in England. It is not quite hardy. I brought home cuttings, but they all died. I have now several plants which I have grown from seed. From their appearance I do not think they will flower well till they are two or three years old; they will want hard cutting back directly after flowering.

(*Later*) That *Iberis* that ornaments French cottage windows and that I called *gibraltarica* is not that at all, but *Iberis semper-virens*. I have one in the greenhouse that was cut back all the

summer and potted up in October. It has been in flower three weeks now, and will go on for a long time. In the Spring I shall cut it well back and plant it out in the reserve garden. It grows easily from cuttings, and Mr Thompson of Ipswich keeps the seed. It is, of course, not a choice plant, but it is an attractive and useful one for those who have not much convenience for forcing on winter flowering things in

December and January. Like many of the commoner plants, I have never seen it grown as a window plant in England, though it would do well.

I have on my flower table a shrubby Begonia in a pot with small, pointed, spotty leaves and hanging white flowers. They are easily reared from seed and I do think they grow so beautifully and can be pruned into such lovely shapes. They are far more beautiful than those great, flat, floppy, opulent, tuberous-rooted ones that flower in the summer. The parent of my plant (mossy green leaves, spotted, silvery-white) must have been called *Begonia alba picta*.

The white Arums which were laid on their side all the summer in the pots and well dried are handsomer plants, and throwing up more flowers than I have ever had before when they were planted out in summer.

In this dry frosty weather we thin and prune out the shrubberies. Every plant is given a fair chance or else cut down. Taking all the suckers from the lilacs improves them immensely. How seldom it is done!

They sell at the Army and Navy Stores an admirable little lamp-stove (Rippingille's patent) for heating small greenhouses. This will keep the frost out of a small house, and is far easier to manage, for an amateur with a gardener who goes home at night, than the usual more expensive arrangement. There are also small forcing boxes to put inside a greenhouse or in a room for bringing on seeds in early Spring.

After a white frost in the morning we have had a day which, except for its shortness, we should be satisfied with and think beautiful in early Spring. These mild, sunny winter days do great harm in prematurely forcing growth, but I know few things which it would be more difficult to wish non-existent. They make up to me for so many of our winter trials – fog and cold and darkness.

I have a plant of *Daphne indica,* one of my favourite Winter flowers, in my greenhouse now. It is in flower and smelling deliciously, but does not look at all satisfactory, although it was only brought last year. It was put out of doors last summer, as it ought to be, but was allowed to get dry. It made no growth, it is leggy, drawn-up and the leaves are yellow, which with hard-wooded plants generally means over-watering in winter. I have tried for years to grow these *Daphnes,* but they are difficult to strike, difficult to grow, and have a quite extraordinary love of dying without any very obvious reason. I must devote myself to finding out, if possible, what the reason is.

(*1899*) In the greenhouse have now been put the first pots of the lovely double *Prunus* with its delicate whiteness of driven snow; no plant forces better. I may have said this, or something like it, before. Never mind; with some plants it is worth while to repeat myself. In the country I do not now care to grow India-rubber plants or Aspidistras, except to give away. They only remind me of towns, and take a good deal of room.

I have in the greenhouse several pots of a white *Oxalis,* I do not know its distinguishing name, with a long growth of its lovely fresh green leaves, which can be picked and mixed with delicate greenhouse flowers, as they last well in water. It has a white flower in Spring and the whole plant is very like an improved version of our wood sorrel, *Oxalis acetosella.*

A tall greenhouse grass called *Cyperus laxus* I find easy to grow. It is very pretty picked in Winter and stuck into a bottle behind some short pieces of bright-coloured flowers. It looks refined, and if against or near white paint or a white wall, its shadows are pretty, thrown by the lamp, through the long evenings.

A greenhouse evergreen called *Rhododendron jasminiflorum* is worth all trouble. It is in bloom now, sweet and graceful and not at all common.

All these half-hardy, hard-wooded plants I find rather difficult to keep in health, but I am going to pay much more attention to their summer treatment. They want to go out for a month or two, but to prevent their getting dry they must be either sunk in coconut fibre or surrounded by moss, or covered with straw. If sunk in the earth, worms are apt to get in. I think they are best replaced towards the middle of August into a cool house, where they can be watched. Sinking the small pot into a larger with some moss between is the best help of all. There is no fun in growing only the things everyone can grow, and nothing vexes me like seeing a plant which came quite healthy from a nurseryman, and in a year not only has not grown, but looks less well than when it first came.

Fate caused me to go to Ireland about this time last year. I dreaded the long night journey and the arrival on the grey Winter morning. But, were the steamers far less splendid seaboats than they are, and the waves every day as stormy as they sometimes are, I think it would be well worth while for any garden-fancier to visit Ireland in January, if only to admire the luxuriant growth of the evergreens and the beauty of the winter-flowering shrubs.

> Mrs Earle had conquered her 'intense physical dread of being on the water' – to some extent, at any rate – years before, when visiting a cousin-by-marriage, the Governor-General of Canada. However '. . . even under the most favourable circumstances, ship life, to me, is odious. You cannot read, you cannot write, you cannot employ yourself in any way. And nearly everyone is bored. Sunday brought the usual Church of England service . . . the hymns "for those at sea" were sung with unusual heartiness'.

In spite of the time of year I had pleasant days in Dublin at the College Botanical Gardens and also at Glasnevin, the Kew of Dublin. The little Irises *stylosa alba* and *speciosa* were flowering well. They must be starved, for if their foliage is good, it means no flowers. Many kinds of Hellebores were coming into bloom, some of which I had never seen before. The warm damp winters are very favourable to January-flowering plants, and we can scarcely expect to copy them in Surrey. The rather rare and interesting *Daphne blagayana* was growing to a great size, and covered the flowers at Glasnevin. In 'The English Flower Garden', Mr Robinson describes it as 'a beautiful dwarf alpine shrub of easy growth'. I have not found it at all easy; in fact, two out of the three plants I had have died, and the third looks rather ill. But I think I tried to grow it too much in the sun; it also wants pegging down every year after flowering.

> The edition of 'The English Flower Garden' to which Mrs Earle referred was the first, published in 1883. Mr Robinson evidently had second thoughts about *D. blagayana's* 'easy growth' as my copy, dated 1906 omits this sentence altogether. Or is there any possibility that Mr Robinson learned something from Mrs Earle?

One of my kind correspondents said she observed I was not so rich in blue flowers as was desirable, and named the following. I mean to get all those I do not already possess. *Commelina coelestis; Anchusa italica; Anchusa capensis; Anchusa sempervirens; Parochetus communis; Phacelia campanularia; Browallia elata; Catananche coerulea; Lenaria retulata; Linaria aureo-purpurea* and *Linaria bipartita; Omphalodes lucilea.*

The French proverb *la variété c'est la vie* always appeals to me in many things, especially domestic ones. I know nothing such a test of a good housekeeper as a periodic change of biscuits. Everybody tires of the best biscuits in the world, and new shapes and qualities should ring the changes. So – all through the summer, a slight surprise and pleasure comes at the end of a little dinner if a buttonhole of sweet-smelling flowers and leaves are carefully tied up and dropped into the water in the finger-bowls. Nothing should be used but what is really sweet – lemon-scented Verbena (and life is always rather unbearable to my luxury-loving nature without lemon-scented Verbena), a little bunch of Violets, Geranium leaves, especially the Prince of Orange, make a combination that pleases everyone.

Last autumn (*1906*) I had a book sent to me called 'Stone Gardens with Practical Hints on the Paving and Planting of them' by Rose Haig Thomas (Simpkins & Marshall). The book rather interested me . . . I think a great deal could be done with making small squares, either in towns or suburbs, much more attractive than they are. Mrs Haig Thomas tells us that to make a stone garden is easy. I do not agree with her. I do not think it is so. Neither is the planting to ensure a really good succession at all easy. Indeed, it would require a good nurseryman in the neighbourhood to supply deficiencies and failures, except in the case of a really large garden where plants can be raised and grown on until wanted in the beds.

One of the occupations connected with this kind of garden is the continual weeding which is necessary, for if weeds and grass get ahead, it looks very ugly and untidy. Lady amateurs generally undertake to do these things themselves, consequently they are often neglected. The whole beauty of a stone garden is spoilt if the borders are not flat and the plants low growing. I cannot say that I think Mrs Haig Thomas's

designs are very satisfactory – not nearly simple enough –
and she is rather fond of banks. Now banks of turf are about
the most difficult and expensive things to keep in good order
in any garden. In nearly all her designs she suggests a water
tank. These also are very difficult to keep clean.

This, with benefit of hindsight, seems to indicate a complete
volte-face by Mrs Earle in the matter of water in the garden.
Ten years earlier she had written that 'a piece of water,
however small . . . is such an added enjoyment to life on a hot
summer's day.' (see page 94) Then, two years later – 'the
(dry) weather makes us doubly appreciate the small square
of cool water just in front of the dining-room window. . .'
Evidently disillusion set in later.

February

On this day last year I went to one of the Drill Hall Horticultural Shows and was especially delighted with *Amygdalus
davidiana*. It is one of the earliest of the flowering shrubs. I
immediately bought a plant, and this year it is in full flower,
every branch wreathed with the lovely delicate white flowers.
I only wish I had bought three or four plants instead of one; I
shall certainly do so next autumn. The branches I ventured
to cut lasted over ten days in the room in water, and those
left on the plant turned brown from the frosty nights.

I returned to 'Woodlands' today after staying some little
time in London. Apart from other reasons, it is worth going
away for the joy of returning. While in London I again went
to the Drill Hall Show some few days later than last year.
Nothing struck me so much this year as the *Amygdalus davidiana* did last year, but it was an especially good show of
flowers for so early in the season. Year by year, the Cycla-
mens grow larger and finer in colour, but I do not think they
are plants that have been greatly improved by increased cultivation and Brobdingnagian size. I prefer the pretty, little
old sweet-smelling types.

I found at home that the Crocuses had made much progress, and the Daffodils, instead of only showing green
spears, are all now in bud. The complete stillness is so delicious to me!!

> How sweet, how passing sweet, is solitude!
> But grant me still a friend in my retreat,
> Whom I may whisper 'Solitude is sweet'. . .

That is what the young feel. The old can do without compan-
ionship.

My little conservatory looked bright and full of bloom.
Last year I had a lot of Daffodils in pans, and they did very
well and forced easily. This year I have Hyacinths but
though they were not very good bulbs, some being successful
and some failures, still they look well and picturesque in the
open pans; far prettier than in pots.

I have one little Oriental slop-basin filled with the bright blue Scillas, which is very effective; and the Freesias are always most satisfactory. Mr Sydenham recommends buying them each year, but I think, cheap as they are, that must be advice rather for the seller than for the buyer, as with us, treated as recommended, they improve and increase, and when there is so much to buy, that is what I call satisfactory.

My large, old-fashioned, sweet-smelling white Azalea, which has been so faithful a friend for many years, has failed, either from mere fatigue or being forced, or from being over-dried and pot-bound last summer, which I think more likely. I have a young plant of the same which is now in full flower – *Azalea indica alba* it is called in the catalogues. But often other varieties are sent out under the same name which have no scent at all, and are consequently much less worth growing in a small greenhouse. My old plant had the most delicious, delicate and yet powerful perfume.

I went to a neighbour today and found the house filled with pots of *Genista praecox*. They came from Waterer's, and a more charming effect in a large room I never saw. The plant was beautifully grown and one mass of pale lemon-coloured bloom, sweet-smelling, too.

There has been in this year's *Guardian*, a succession of monthly papers on a Surrey garden, written by Miss Jekyll of Munstead Wood, Godalming. I give her address, as she now sells her surplus plants, all more or less suited to light soils, to the management of which she has for many years past given special attention. These papers have much illuminating matter in them, and are called 'Notes from Garden and Woodlands'. I trust that before long these articles will be re-published in book form, for every word in them deserves attention and consideration.

> Mrs Earle was delighted when, in February 1899, these articles were indeed re-published by Longmans, Green & Co. Ltd. in book form, under the title 'Wood and Garden'. In 1982 the book was re-issued by the Antique Collectors' Club.

A treat has come for all of us amateur gardeners this month in the publication of a long looked-for gardening book by Miss Jekyll, charmingly illustrated from photographs of her own.

But, good as are these reproductions, in my opinion they can never compare with woodcuts or steel engravings, and they give but a faint idea of the unusual charm and beauty of her self-created garden. Her book is most truly called 'Wood and Garden' and is a never-ending lesson of how to lay out a piece of ground by using its natural advantages instead of hopelessly destroying them by clearing the ground to make a garden. But the charm of the combination of nature and art as carried out by Miss Jekyll is very great. All the plants and flowers about which she writes she actually grows on the top of her Surrey hill. Her garden is a most instructive one, and encouraging, too. She has gone through the stage, so common to all ambitious and enthusiastic amateurs, of trying to grow everything, and of often wasting much precious room in growing inferior plants, or plants which, even though they may be worth growing in themselves, are yet not worth the care and feeding which a light soil necessitates if they are to be successful.

> This last comment of Mrs Earle's is frequently quoted out of context, so making it seem to be a prickly, if not actually barbed, shaft aimed at Miss Jekyll. The following passages, of course, counteract any such interpretation.

This, to me, rather delightful characteristic of amateurs in every art was severely condemned by Mr Ruskin in my youth, when he said that the amateur sketcher always attempted to draw the panorama of Rome on his thumb-nail instead of humbly trying to reproduce what was at his own door. The practice is just as common in gardening as in music and painting.

Every plant she (*Miss Jekyll*) names is worth getting and growing in gardens that are of considerable size, and which more or less share her Surrey soil and climate.

Miss Jekyll says: 'There is always, in February, some one day at least when one smells the yet distant, coming summer'. Such a day has been ours today, and I enjoyed it doubly in consequence of having so lately returned from London. And the forwardness of the spring – it really is more forward even than last year – makes one enjoy it more, though everything is growing so fast, it is quite agitating for the gardener, giving the feeling that all the work is behindhand. I am told that many have thought I recommend that things should be done too soon; but in my experience human nature rather tends to reversing the proverb, and acts on the principle of Never do today what can be done tomorrow. And in all things about the garden, except when Jack Frost is to be feared, it is best to be early rather than late.

> There can be no question that Theresa Earle was a sincere admirer of Gertrude Jekyll, her garden and her manifold accomplishments. She was also, although she never says so,

acquainted with her. It would have been strange if she were not. They were County neighbours, only seven years apart in age and had shared interests in art, music, embroidery, as well as gardening; they also had friends in common.

Sir Herbert Jekyll, Gertrude's brother, and with whom she lived, had been very active in furthering the career of Theresa's son, Lionel, who wrote in his autobiography 'He (Sir Herbert) and his charming wife (Lady Agnes) were friends of my parents, and it was to him that I owe everything in life as regards my career'.

It has to be remembered, too, that that close friend and colleague of Gertrude Jekyll's, Edwin Lutyens, was a relative by marriage of Mrs Earle, having married her niece, Emily Lytton. They were a close-knit family, traditionally helpful to each other. Mrs Earle must have known the young Ned Lutyens, and that she took an interest in his career is suggested in a remark in one of her letters from Munich in 1905 . . . 'How I wish Ned would come here; there are lots of buildings which I think would interest him'. So it seems not unlikely – at least, it is interesting to speculate – that, as Mrs Earle had herself acknowledged the help of all her friends in 'pushing' her own first book, there might well be something of the *quid pro quo* in her praising and publicising Gertude's writings.

As I rush about the garden and see how the daffies grow an inch each day in such weather, in spite of the very cold nights, and though I have the usual endless 'Martha-ish' bothers of life inside the house, I can indeed say with Thomson:

> I care not, Fortune, what you me deny!
> You cannot rob me of free nature's grace,
> You cannot shut the windows of the sky
> Through which Aurora shows her bright'ning face.
> You cannot bar my constant feet to trace
> The woods and lawns by living stream at eve
> Let health my nerves and finer fibres brace,
> And I their toys to the great children leave.
> Of fancy, reason, virtue, nought can me bereave.

Through the year, books on natural history and gardening must be our constant companions to be any real good. We must verify for ourselves what the book tells us. This greatly increases the interest of life in the country and no one is ever dull or bored who can learn about plants.

I know, alas, that to those who really love to dwell in towns it is no use speaking of such things. The poetry of life is never to be seen by them out of the streets (*sic*); and children brought up in large towns rarely acquire a love of the country, I think. I remember, when we were children, a friend who came from London to see us used to tell us she could not say her prayers in the country – it was so dreadfully still! Fancy missing to that extent the city's noise, the rattle of the cabs down the streets or the measured tread of feet along the pavement.

In these days, garden cities are growing up in many directions and becoming more and more popular. I wondered, when driving through one of these, how it would be for those coming out of a great smoky town, and knowing nothing of the country; what they would do, and how they would manage to make beautiful and utilise the small plots of ground allotted to them; how they would know how to turn their bare walls and palings into something beautiful and so add to the interest of their lives by understanding how to cultivate what would grow around them.

Sixteen years after writing this, Mrs Earle and her friend Ethel Case set about assisting 'those coming out of a great smoky town into the country' by collaborating on a book for the rawest of beginners, with the uninviting title 'Gardening for the Ignorant'. In her introduction she wrote:

It seems a most preposterous idea that, with all the number of garden books, large and small, good and bad, dear and cheap, that have been published of late, I should still feel there is a want and that I should try to supply it. The fact is that none of those books that I have seen begins quite enough at the beginning, and they pre-suppose a knowledge that many are without. My friend, Ethel Case, who last year had to arrange and plant a garden of her own in Hampshire, discovered that her ignorance of the vegetable garden was very difficult to dispel, all the books she consulted gave vague directions but none took the anxious, groping amateur by the hand to lead him over the first most difficult stage.

Catalogues are hardly less puzzling, with their long lists of varieties and fancy names, and the garden terminology which is unintelligible to people who are town-bred. So my friend and I decided that we would write a book together, I with my greater experience, she with practical knowledge from doing work herself.

A collector of old books has objected to my great praise of *'Les Roses'* by Redouté. He says 'I do not attach the same value to it that you do, and have never found it of much use, as nearly all the roses are hybrids and varieties, many of which have passed away'. I was no doubt mistaken, but my impression was that the lovely illustrations represent in

many instances the wild roses of the world, which have ceased to be cultivated, but which could easily be produced again from seed by those who took the trouble. My correspondent goes on to describe a book – which I had never seen – that treats of all the wild roses of the world. He says 'You should get a coloured copy of Lindley's "Monograph of Roses", 1819. It is an excellent book, both as to plates and descriptions, and though not common, is cheap. You can see them all at Kew.'

I have now succeeded in procuring, through my Frankfort friend, a coloured copy of *'Rosarum Monographia'* by John Lindley (London) 1820. The letterpress is far more interesting and instructive, but the actual artistic treatment of the plates is less beautiful and delicate than Redouté's.

Where people suffer much from the birds eating out buds, as I do, I strongly recommend picking some of the branches of *Prunus pissardi* when in bud, and sticking them into Japanese wedges or into ordinary glass vases. This, insofar as house decoration is concerned, defeats the bullfinches, and the buds come out very well in the room. This is the same with all the early flowering blossoms. The pink Almond and *Pyrus japonica* are far more lovely flowered in water in a warm room than left on the trees exposed to the cold nights and the nipping east wind.

Although present-day flower arrangers might not appreciate Mrs Earle's phraseology – 'sticking' Prunus into containers – she was an early enthusiast for this particular art form. Her niece, Lady Constance Lytton (she of the measles, see page 9) added an Appendix to the first 'Pot-pourri' on the 'Japanese Art of Arranging Cut Flowers', demonstrating how 'this artistic science may be adapted to English flowers and English drawing-rooms.'

March

Such a lovely Spring day, in spite of its cold wind! It makes me long to be sixteen miles away in my little garden. Even here in London, great pure white stately clouds are sailing over the blue. How lucky I am to be going away so soon. I wish it gave half as much pleasure to the rest of the family as it does to me; but one of the few advantages of old age is that we may be innocently selfish.

(*Woodlands*) March is the great seed-sowing month. There is no more delightful occupation to the true gardener than sowing seeds on the right sort of day, seeing all the time, through the power of imagination, the show they will make in the summer. The creative instinct is strong in all of us, and the feeling that without our work the ground would be bare and that it is our privilege to help Nature to complete her work fills one with an overwhelming sense of the wonder of it all. Besides this the day itself, the real seed-sowing day, which is worth waiting for, is in itself the best day of the year; mild, slightly damp, still and sunny; the grass has begun to grow, the first shoots of Crown Imperials, Lupins, Campanulas, Paeonies and other early plants are showing; the rooks, if there are any in the country, will come and caw to you, above all the smell of Spring which is more than any other the cleanest, most delightful, soul-satisfying of scents. It is indeed a day to be looked forward to all the winter.

I have had two real good days' gardening, and have tried to carry out some of Miss Jekyll's hints, even in this commonplace, everyday garden. I have pulled down some of the climbing Roses, to let them make low-growing bushes, for it is so true that, as she says, when planted on a pergola all their beauty is only for the bird as it flies.

In the lanes, too, I saw some of the wild Arum leaves, and got out of the carriage to get some. Having no garden-gloves or knife with me, I ran my fingers down into the soft leafy mould to gather them with the white stalk underground. I trust these will rejoice an invalid friend in London tomorrow. One gets almost tired of the mass of flowers in London now and things that smell of ditches and hedgerows are what one values most.

I spoke of pergolas – those covered walks made with poles, or columns of bricks or stone, and overgrown with creepers of all kinds. Now I would speak of the 'Charmilles', walks either of turf or gravel covered over with arches of growing trees with no supports of wires or wood, merely the interlacing of the boughs till they grow thick overhead with continual pruning. There is a little short walk of this kind at Hampton Court – I forget how it is made (I mean, with what trees it is planted), and in the Boboli Gardens at Florence there are endless varieties of these covered walks. They would be very beautiful on the north or east side of many a sunny lawn; and if a garden were too small for such a walk, there might still be room for an occasional self-forming arch, which adds mystery and charm to any garden.

> The 'Charmille' at Hampton Court is on the Privy Garden and referred to as Queen Mary's Bower. This was originally planted by Henry VIII for Anne Boleyn, re-made during the reign of William and Mary (hence the name) in wych elm. This succumbed to Dutch elm disease, and the present planting is of hornbeam.

The lion-like character of the weather is softening and all the little spring things are through. Each day makes a difference, but the delightful feeling of new life is already everywhere. Our reason tells us this is because Nature has been asleep, not dead. There is no mistake about the poor really dead plants; we know them too well. Early spring here is not beautiful at all; it is dry and shrivelled and hard-looking, not like the neighbourhood of my old home by the Hertfordshire millstream.

This is the first Spring morning. How one appreciates the slightest rise in the temperature. I quite pity those who have rushed South, and who cannot watch the slow development of our English Spring with all its many disappointments. The bright yellow flowers of the improved Tussilago coltsfoot are now just coming out, and the gravelly corner where they grow is a bright mass of buds. These flowers that come before their leaves, like the Autumn Crocus, are attractive, though the size of their leaves, when they do come, puts one sometimes out of conceit with them, especially if crowded for room; though it is astonishing how corners can be found in even small gardens for all sorts of things, if one gives the matter constant attention. Having everything under one's eye, one never forgets to notice how they get on.

My garden is now full of the old wild sweet Violet, *Violet odorata* of our youth, before even the Czars came in, much less the giant new kinds. I have always rather snorted at the modern large Violets, because I cannot succeed with them, and because they are so different from the much-loved ones of my youth. But I must own that, when grown to perfection, in soil of the strength and moisture loved by the cabbage tribe, in full sun, the 'Princess of Wales' is a splendid variety, and has a sweet violet smell when first picked. I must try again, across the kitchen-garden, in soil as rich as I can make it, and then trust to the wet summers we are supposed to be going to have.

I have an immense affection for the (wild) Violet, with its beautiful intense colour and its delicate perfume. It grew all about the Hertfordshire garden under the hedges and little seedlings started up in the gravel paths, looking bold and defiant, but all the same they were rooted out by the gardener when summer tidying began.

At the end of March, or early April, when the rain comes, I divide up and plant bits of these Violets everywhere, and they grow and flourish and increase under gooseberry bushes and currant bushes, along the palings covered with blackberries, under shrubs, anywhere, in fact, and there they remain, hidden and shaded and undisturbed all the summer. Where seedlings appear they are let alone all the summer and autumn till after flowering time in spring. They look lovely and brave these cold, dry March days, but their stalks are rather short here, for want of moisture. If anyone wants

This Grave

YOUNG ENGLISH POET

"Here lies One
Whose Name was Writ in Water."
1795-1821

to see this Violet to perfection, let him chance to be in Rome early in March, as I once was, and let him go to the old English cemetery where Keats lies buried and the heart of Shelley, and he will see a never-to-be-forgotten sight – the whole ground blue with the Violets, tall and strong above their leaves, the air one sweet perfume, and the sound, soft and yet distinct, of the murmur of Spring bees.

I (*knew*) Lady Shelley, the wife of Sir Percy, the only surviving son of the poet; they lived in one of the beautiful new houses on the Chelsea Embankment. The book she published in 1859, called 'Shelley's Memorials', was at that time the only true and authentic account of the life and death of Shelley. Lady Shelley was an enthusiast, and I used always to feel that marriages take place for many reasons, but to marry for the sake of a dead father-in-law is one, at any rate, that is unusual.

Evidently young romantics find the combination of flower, scent and Keats as irresistible today as did Mrs Earle nearly a century ago. Owing to their depredations, the wild violets

47

need to be replaced yearly – as indeed they are, with under-standing forgiveness, by the London-based Keats-Shelley Memorial Association.

This is the first year I have forced *Spiraea confusa,* and it makes a lovely pot plant. We left it out in the cold till the middle of January. In forcing all hardy things, that is the great secret; send them to sleep as early as you can by taking them up and exposing them to cold. All plants must have their rest. The leaves of this *Spiraea* are a blue-grey, and the branches are wreathed with miniature May blossoms. Alas, they do not do well picked and in water.

Mustard and cress, much grown in boxes in early Spring, and which is so delicious at five o'clock tea or with bread and butter and cheese, many people will not eat because it is often gritty. This certainly makes it horrid, and if the cress is washed it makes it very wet, often without getting rid of the grit.

The best way to grow it is to make the earth very damp be-fore sowing, press it down flat, and then sow the seed very lightly on the top, making a division between the mustard and cress. Cover it with a tile, or something else to make it dark, till it has sprouted, and then cut it carefully straight into the plate or small fancy basket in which it is to be served, without washing it at all. If grown in this way, and carefully cut, there will be no grit whatever. I find small, low, round, Japanese baskets of various sizes (from Liberty's) are most useful in a house with a garden. They are beautifully made and very pretty, and fruit can be picked into them at once, and served whether at breakfast or luncheon without any fingering in the pantry or kitchen.

I must begin to tell you about my old garden books, and how I first came to know about them, and then to collect them. Until lately I was absolutely ignorant of their exist-ence, and had never seen an illustrated flower book of the last century. About fifteen years ago I was living in London, with apparently small prospect of ever living in the country again, or of ever possessing a garden of my own. When 'A Year in a Lancashire Garden' by Henry A. Bright was published in 1879, the book charmed me, and I thought it simple, unaffected and original. 'A Year in a Lancashire Garden' has been much imitated, but, to my mind, none of the imitations possess the charm of the original. It is a fascinating chat about a garden to read in a town and dream over, as I did. It revived in me, almost to longing, the old wish to have a garden, and I resolved, if it were ever realised,

that every plant named by Henry Bright I would get and try to grow. This I literally carried out when I came to live in Surrey. His joys have been my joys, and his failures have sometimes been mine, too.

In the 'Lancashire Garden' I was delighted to find a sentence which exactly expressed an opinion I had long held, but never met with in words before. As I agree with it even more strongly now than I did then, it is well I should quote it here, for the evil it denounces exists still, not only in England but even more in several countries I have visited abroad:

'For the ordinary bedding-out of ordinary gardens I have a real contempt. It is at once gaudy and monotonous. A garden is left bare for eight months in the year, that for the four hottest months there shall be a blaze of the hottest colours. The same combination of the same flowers appears wherever you go – Calceolarias, Verbena, Zonal Pelargoniums, with a border of Pyrethrums or Cerastiums; and that is about all. There is no thought and no imagination.'

Yet, twenty years ago, this sort of garden was like Tory politics, or Church and State, and seemed to represent all that was considered respectable and desirable. I shall never forget the bombshell I seemed to fling into a family circle when I injudiciously and vehemently said that I *hated* parks and bedded-out gardens!

What is of chief interest about Joseph Paxton (1803-65) is that he was the greatest unconscious instrument in the movement he helped to develop, which altered the gardening of the whole of England, and consequently of the world (*bedding-out*). Endless sums of money were at his disposal and everything was done which could facilitate his efforts to make the terraces of Chatsworth a blaze of colour during the months of August and September, the months when his master was at home. It was copied, for the same reason, by most of the great houses in England. But what was really unfortunate, and can only recall the old fable of the ox and the frog, was the imitation of this system in all the gardens of England, down to the half-acre surrounding a vicarage, or the plot of ground in front of a suburban residence. The ox, as we know, was big by nature; and when the frog imitated him, it was flattering to the ox, but the frog came to grief. So I think to this day, if bedding-out is ever tolerable, it is on the broad terraces facing large stone houses, with which we have nothing to do here.

Where it becomes intolerable, and perhaps it is hard to blame Paxton for this, is in the miniature Chatsworths, with their little lawns and their little beds, their Pelargoniums, often only coloured leaves like Mrs Pollock, their dwarf Calceolarias, their purple Verbenas and their blue Lobelias; where the lady is not allowed to pick, and where the gardener, if he is masterful and gets his own way, turns the old herbaceous border in front of the house into that terrible abomination called carpet bedding.

Paxton was a very remarkable man in his way. When taken up by the Queen and the Prince Consort, he built in 1851 the wonderful and ever-to-be-remembered glass case in Hyde Park, the first general International Exhibition, which enclosed two large elms. Poor trees, how they hated it! Their drooping autumnal appearance is my strongest childish remembrance of that Exhibition. I do not remember feeling that anyone really admired it, or indeed the various exhibits. It was a peculiarly ugly time all over Europe for dress, furniture, china, glass &c. All this was so marked in everyone's recollection that 'early Victorian' has become synonymous with young people for bad taste and vulgar ostentation. The excessive fatigue and weariness so stamped on the face of everybody who wanders about huge exhibitions became at that time a source of amusement for the London street boy, and took the form of calling out as they passed 'How's your poor feet?' I imagine that this exhibition did a great deal towards levelling luxury and spreading a certain kind of civilisation throughout Europe. Telegraphs and railroads have done the rest.

The first edition of Robinson's 'The Wild Garden' was published in 1881, and of all modern illustrated flower-books it is the only one I know that makes me feel really enthusiastic. The drawings in it, by Mr Alfred Parsons, are exquisite and quite original. At the time of its publication the method was new, and, to my mind, it has not yet been surpassed. I have also the fourth edition, which came out in 1894, with much new matter and several new illustrations, especially landscapes; but I prefer the first edition – perhaps because we get fond of the particular edition that originally gave pleasure.

I am afraid that the hopeful instructions on 'wild gardening' so cheerfully laid down by Mr Robinson must be taken with a great many grains of salt when it comes to putting them into practice, especially in dry soil. With care, labour, knowledge and space, exquisite gardens may be laid out, suitable to the various soils of England; but, in my experience, even the best planting goes off without renewal of the soil. This shows itself with the happy possessors of these so-called 'wild gardens' by the constant desire to extend them into pastures new. All I wish to point out is that merely buying the plants and sticking them in does not make a wild garden. The first essentials are space and isolation; they are worth nothing, if crowded.

Of all the many catalogues I receive, none, I think, is produced with anything like the attractive intelligence of the one sent out by Messrs. Ware of Tottenham. This year, one is tempted to say, from the pretty European-Japanese drawing on the cover, that Nature made a mistake in not giving us sometimes an all-over pink sky instead of a blue one! The soil at Tottenham is very heavy, and plants that flourish admirably there, from my experience, unfortunately decline altogether to grow when removed to a purer air and a lighter soil. A visit to Messrs. Ware's garden, as well as constantly going to Kew, will show amateurs what can be done. The old-fashioned idea that a garden meant a place of quiet and repose is not the proper mental attitude for suburban plant-cultivators!

I never refuse to name anything I like when I am told 'Everyone knows that', for 'everyone' is a very limited London circle, where bright, pretty things come like beautiful bubbles, are seen by what is called 'everybody' and are gone in a moment. I think of my kind unknown friends who are far away, bearing the white woman's burden, and who have written to me saying they enjoyed the little breath of home my books have brought them. They may not have seen or heard what I have, and even here in Surrey I find that often the thing that 'everyone knows' does not even reach the next parish.

Yesterday, I paid a visit to the Horticultural College at Swanley, with its branch for women students. It immediately struck me as quite possible that a new employment may be developed for women of small means out of the modern increased taste for gardening. In many of the suburban districts the dullness of the small plots of ground in front of the houses is entirely owing to the want of education in the neighbouring nurserymen, whose first idea is always to plant laurels or other coarse shrubs. The owners of such villas have little time to attend to the garden themselves. A Lady gardener might easily undertake to lay out these plots in endless variety, supplying them through the year with flowers and plants suited to the aspect of each garden. The smaller the space the more necessary the knowledge of what is likely to succeed. Another opening may be found in cases of larger villas, where single ladies might prefer a woman head-gardener with a man under her to do the rougher and heavier work. The maintaining of a garden and the tending of a greenhouse is work particularly suited to women of a certain age. A small greenhouse never can be productive of flowers for picking through the dull months without a great deal of thought, care and knowledge.

> Some ten years after writing this, Mrs Earle became a patron, with Gertrude Jekyll, of the College of Gardening (for women) at Glynde, Sussex, run by Viscountess Wolseley. But her enthusiasm for careers for women didn't end with gardening.

Soon after I came to London I joined the Committee of the Society in Berners Street for promoting the employment of women. . . . It insisted especially, and does still, on the training of girls, for though things have improved, parents are very neglectful of giving young girls an education that fits them to earn their living, and this applies to all classes alike. It is criminal selfishness for a father with a fair income, but unable to provide for his daughters after his death, not to leave them already started in a wage-earning profession.

I do not vouch for the absolute correctness of the following statements, but I find them among my notes, and I think there is some truth in them:

Lettuce is calming and beneficial to anyone suffering from insomnia.

Honey is wholesome, strengthening, cleansing, healing and nourishing.

Lemons afford relief to feverish thirst in sickness and, mixed with hot water, are a help in biliousness, low fever, colds, coughs, rheumatism, etc.

In cases of disease of the nerves and nervous dyspepsia, tomatoes are a powerful aperient for the liver and are invaluable in all conditions of the system in which the use of calomel is indicated.

Onions are useful in cases of nervous prostration, and will quickly relieve and tone up a worn-out system. They are also useful in all cases of coughs, colds and influenza.

Apples are nutritious, medicinal and vitalising. They aid digestion, clear the voice and correct acidity of the stomach.

Couch grass, the gardener's enemy, from its habit of creeping underground in the Spring, makes a most wholesome 'tisane' for children and rheumatic and gouty people; a handful of the grass, roots and all, must be well washed and thrown into a pint of boiling water and boiled for ten minutes, and then strained. Black currant leaves treated in the same way are equally good for clearing the blood in Autumn.

(Personal) The following suggestion is worth knowing for anybody who has a bilious headache and is obliged to make a speech, or any great effort. Put a

whole tin of Colman's mustard into a large hot bath,
stay in it ten or fifteen minutes, lie down after it for half
an hour. The brain will then be far clearer and better
than in ordinary health. This is a remedy only to be
used for an emergency. It is, of course, rather a severe
trial for the circulation, but less likely to be injurious
than the drugs which are so often taken for headaches.

In the old convent gardens, Calvary Clover was supposed
not to grow unless sown on Good Friday. It is a curious little
annual, with a blood-red spot on each leaf, and the seed-pod
is surrounded by a case which pulls out, or rather unwinds,
into a miniature crown of thorns.

This is one of the 'common names' that turn out to be anything but common. William Robinson describes Calvary
Clover as 'the common name of a pretty variety of the white
Dutch clover, in which the leaves are almost entirely of a
deep bronze-purple colour' Botanist Raymond Clarke, MA
thought it could be *Trifolium stellatum*, or possibly *Trifolium
pratense*. Chelsea Physic Garden thought *Medicago Arabica*, the
Spotted Medick – and so did I. We all now agree – almost
completely – with the Natural History Museum, who identify
it as *Medicago Echinus*. I conclude it may be a matter of individual choice; but my thanks to Mr Clarke, to Alan Burman
and Virginia Nightingale at the Chelsea Physic Garden and
to the Natural History Museum for their endless trouble.

I read with regret the other day in a leading evening newspaper of the authoritative revival of the notion that eating
tomatoes is the cause of the increase of cancer. This theory
seems likely to deprive the poorer public of one of the best
and cleanest blood-purifiers within reach of the inhabitants
of our towns. The population of the whole south of Europe
has eaten tomatoes from time immemorial. Would it not be
far more sensible to look for the cause of cancer in the great
increase of meat-eating, especially in towns, the over-fed and
diseased cattle, tinned and other preserved animal food, and
the much-consumed modern stimulant, beef-tea?

Three years before writing this, Mrs Earle had been recommending 'Dainty Dishes' by Lady Harriet Sinclair, a cookery book of which she said 'I have known it all my married life, and have found no other book on cooking so useful, so clear, or in such good taste'. Lady Harriet's recipe for beef tea calls for 3 lbs. of beef, with bones, chopped; carrots, turnips, celery, onion or leeks, salt, pepper and sugar, simmered, skimmed and strained. 'Very good to drink cold during the night for invalids' said Lady Harriet.

April

Early Spring; Petroleum Tubs; 'The English Flower Garden'; Old mill by the River Mole; Mr Burbidge on Fragrant Leaves and Flowers; Letter on night-flowering flowers; Butterflies and moths; A Week in France; Cactuses; Shortage of Vegetables; Mangold wurzels; Poultry.

Nothing, I think, tempts me so much to neglect all duties and to forget all ties as gardening in early spring weather. Everything is of such a great importance and the rush of work that one feels ought to be done without a moment's delay makes it, to me at least, feel the most necessary thing in life.

A friend wrote to me once: 'The best thing in old age is to care for nothing but Nature, our real old mother, who will never desert us, and who opens her arms to us every spring and summer again, warm and young as ever, till at last we lie dead in her breast.'

Another wrote: 'Serenity, serenity, serenity and light. Surely this is the atmosphere of Olympus; and if we cannot attain to it in age, in vain has our youth gone through the passionate toil and struggle of its upward journey to the divine summits.'

These thoughts fit better the solitude of bursting woods in the real country than the cultivating mania in a small garden, where we are all tempted to fight against Erasmus's assertion – one piece of ground will not hold all sorts of plants.

The uses of petroleum tubs in a garden are endless. I get my oil now from London and so do not return the barrels. Mr Barr told me the other day he was knocking the bottoms out of some, sinking them one below the other with a pipe in between, and puddling them with stiff clay at the bottom; then he was going to plant them with specimens of the beautiful new French *nymphaes* (water lilies) – M. Marliac's hybrids being the most beautiful perhaps, of all. A full, excellent and detailed account of the cultivation of these water lilies is to be found in Mr Robinson's last edition of 'The English Flower Garden'. As is natural at my age, I have a most elderly affection for types and parent plants, because as a rule they are less expensive to buy, and much more willing to be managed when one has got them. But I do not say this without, from my heart, giving all honour to cultivators of hybrid plants.

Tub arrangements can be made of endless use even in the smallest gardens and backyards if sunny – never forgetting the precious rain water, which every slight slope in the ground makes it easy to collect, if the tubs are sunk level with the ground. I mention things again and again, knowing well in our full modern lives how useful it is merely to remind.

We have walked this evening down to the old mill by the river Mole. I have, not unnaturally, a great affection for a watermill, as I passed all my childhood so close to its thumping mysteries, and my bedroom as a girl was just above the rushing mill-tail, where the brown trout lay under the laurels. My old mill is all modernised and altered now, while here the miller says with pride 'I have been here fifty-two years, and I grind the flour with the old stones – no modern china rollers for me.' We buy his flour and his wholemeal and his bran. The latter is what we really went down to fetch, as one of my nieces is fond of bran water. This wildly stimulating beverage – far too much a tonic for my age – is

an American drink. You pour cold water on two handfuls of fresh bran, let it stand for four hours, and then pour it off. It is supposed to contain some of the phosphates in the husks of the wheat, and consequently has much of the nourishing qualities of brown bread.

Last year at this time I was able to go and hear, at the Drill Hall, Westminster, Mr Burbidge's exceedingly interesting address on Fragrant Leaves and Sweet-smelling Flowers. This lecture has since been published in the journal of the Horticultural Society for October, 1896.

Beyond wishing to remind others how much pleasure and instruction one gets from being a Fellow of the Royal Horticultural Society, I take a section from his lecture which seems useful and desirable for all gardeners. He says:

'I want you to rate all fragrant foliage quite as highly as you now profess to value sweet-scented blossoms. I also want to point out some of the essential differences, and advantages even, of foliage leaves as opposed to those floral leaves we call flowers. I am also particularly anxious to try and show that there is a sanitary basis, rather than a merely sensuous reason, for the usage of sweet odours and vegetable perfumes, whether the same be fresh or dried, living, dead or distilled. Modern researches have amply proved that ozone is developed when the sun shines on most kinds of fragrant plants, such as flowers, fir and pine trees, and sweet herbs generally.'

It is not much trouble to sow lemon pips, and yet what is more delicious and reviving than the crushed leaf of a lemon tree? I have found my increased number of rosemary bushes a great joy. They live everywhere with the slightest protection – namely, stuffed in all sorts of places under shrubs. But to grow and flower to perfection, as they do in Italy, they want to be under a wall in a warm corner, and fairly well-nourished. No doubt their tendency to be killed in hard springs in the open must be the reason that so many gardens, especially small ones, where they are most precious, are content to do without them.

Another very interesting letter I have received, I will quote:

> 'I am simply writing with the object of calling your attention to a group of plants which I have in my small way been cultivating for years, and which give me great pleasure every summer. I refer to the night-flowering and night-scented plants. To a business-man like myself they are specially welcome, as my time is all occupied with business during the day, and the evening only is left in which we can enjoy our gardens. The most interesting in the group is that exquisite little gem of an annual, *Schizopetalum Walkeri*. It has no English name, unfortunately. This little flower is pure ivory white, of a Maltese cross form, and after dark throws out a most delicate perfume, not unlike the Almond. I also sow a packet or two of *Matthiola bicornis* or Sweet-scented stock . . . *Nicotiana affinis* . . . *Hesperis tristis* . . . *Oenothera odora*. So here you have a small group of plants which kindly reserve their fragrance, store it up during the day-time, and then considerately, during the twilight and evening when the breadwinner of the family comes home after his day's toil, throw out their precious odours and make the garden all the pleasanter and more refreshing for the nightly stroll after supper.'

Schizopetalum Walkeri has now acquired the English name 'stamp flower'. It is described by Louise B. Wilder as having blossoms like little squares of white lace scented with almonds.

I cannot understand anybody living in the country and not taking a special interest in wild birds, from the skylark, the smallest bird that soars, to the water wagtail, the smallest bird that walks. The constant fight always goes on as to whether birds in a garden do good or harm. Nothing convinces my gardener that we do not suffer more than our neighbours from the non-killing of bullfinches. Poor little things – the harm they do is terribly more apparent than the good, which has to be taken on faith – and this I do.

We started today to spend a week in a French country house, sleeping one night on our way at beautiful Chartres, which, as I am not writing a guide book, I shall not describe. The weather was bitterly cold; and when we humbly asked at the hotel for some hot water, the answer we got was *'On n'échauffe plus'*. The French submit more meekly than we do to this kind of regulation, which is curious, as they are so much more sensible, as a rule, than we are in most of the details of life.

I was interested to see in the small court of the hotel a quantity of most flourishing *Hepaticas*. These flowers, Mr Bright tells us, defeated all his efforts in his Lancashire

garden. I have tried them in various aspects, but they make a sorry show with me in Surrey. In this little backyard they shone in the sunshine, pink and blue, double and single. I suppose the secret is that they do not mind cold, but they want sun. I wonder if anyone is very successful with them in England?

My old books taught me to take an interest in cactuses, which in the early part of the century were much grown. They are very easy of cultivation, and well worth growing for those who spend June and July in their gardens. A succession must be aimed at, as the drawback is that the blooms only last a short time.

The old *Cereus speciosissimum* surpasses in beauty and splendour any garden plant I know, with its brilliant scarlet petals shot with the richest purple and its handsome white tassel of stamens.

Another beautiful flower is the large white night-flowering *Cereus;* if brought, when just about to bloom, into the hall or sitting-room, its delicious perfume pervades the whole house for twenty-four hours, if not for longer.

Although cactuses are very easy to cultivate, yet what they require they must have, or they do not flower at all, and then gardeners throw them away. Wholesome neglect is better than too much misdirected care; they want to be kept very dry, and not too warm all through the winter, but quite free from frost. In April they are re-potted, if they seem to require it, but that is seldom. Once started into growth, they want heat, light, sun, a little nourishment and plenty of watering and syringing, with rain water if possible.

From the point of view of a real Cactus lover, I am but a weak-kneed disciple. I confess that a greenhouse full of these plants in various stages of bumpiness and without a single flower, as is often the case, leaves me cold and rather depressed. But to grow a certain number is of very great interest to me. The power they have of clinging to life is shared by few plants. This accounts for the fact that some of the finest kinds may be seen occasionally in cottage windows. The most gratifying point about cottage window gardening is that, in it, fashion is unknown. Plants have been handed down, from father to son, with a total disregard as to whether these are fashionable or not. For a lengthened period cactuses have been a neglected family. Just lately, magnificent groups have been exhibited by London nurserymen, so they are fast coming to the front again.

Since writing my last book I have learnt by experience a good deal more about Cactus culture. Like all distinct plant families in nature, the more we know about cactuses the more interesting they are. In this country they require a kind of double treatment, according to whether you want them to grow or to flower. If you want small pieces to grow quickly, you must keep them most of the year in heat and well-watered. If, on the other hand, and this especially applies to the hardier kinds, you want them to flower, you must starve them well through the winter. But I am sure that allowing them to shrivel from want of water is wrong. To prevent this, once the year is turned, I find occasional syringing better than much watering at the roots. Over-watering in winter generally means death, as they then rot at the corm. Sun they must have, all through the summer.

One of my correspondents was exceedingly sceptical about the same bloom of my night-flowering *Cereus* having lasted in a cool dark hall for two nights. But it certainly did. Last year I was away from home all the precious summer months, so I do not know what happened to the 'bright blooming *Cereus*, grand and glorious'. Cactus have a way of flowering when they choose. They will not wait for you if you are away, and their blooms only last a short time; but when they do condescend to flower, the beauty of them is exquisite, far more rare and lovely than any orchid that I know.

I have a great many *Stapelias*, South African plants rather resembling miniature cactuses in their growth, and requiring the same treatment. They are very curious, and described as belonging to a group of plants called 'indoloid'. Sometimes the scent of these South African *Stapelias* resembles that of decomposing mammalian flesh, sometimes of rotten fish, etc. This, of course, attracts insects. Flowers provided with indoloid scents resemble animal corpses in their colouring, having usually livid spots, violet streaks and red brown veins on a greenish or a fawn-coloured background. All the same, the flowers are to me curious and rather beautiful, so entirely unlike anything else.

The three or four weeks of severe frosty weather in March made us very short of vegetables. I never buy when I have not guests, as feeling the pinch makes one alive to one's deficiencies, and causes one to manage better another year. So I thought I would try and see how I liked the root we grow for the cows. We have plenty left, as the winter has been so mild. It is Sutton's Mangold Wurzel, a yellow kind. We boiled it till tender, whole, like a beetroot, and when hot cut it into slices, and ate it with cold butter. It was excellent. In texture, it was like a beetroot, in taste half like a sweet potato, half like a chestnut. When mangolds are young they mash like turnips.

Early this month Hops began to show through the ground. When the shoots are about six or eight inches high, before the leaves develop, they can be picked, tied together in a bundle, and cooked exactly like green asparagus. They have not much taste, but are pleasant in substance and are supposed, on the Continent to be exceedingly wholesome.

Since their introduction by the Romans, hops eaten as a vegetable have slid up and down the social scale. John Bickerdyke, writing in 1889, said 'the poorer classes in some parts of Europe still eat the young hops as a vegetable.' Even earlier, Nicholas Culpeper in his 'Complete Herbal' advocated hops, boiled and served up like asparagus, as 'a very wholesome as well as a pleasant tasted spring food. They purify the blood and keep the body gently open'. Today, the English Tourist Board's 'English Food and Drink' suggests

May-picked shoots of the hop as a rare delicacy, occasionally available, served hot, covered in melted butter.

I am often asked what my vegetable seed bill amounts to. The fact is, I never know. Seeds are so cheap that I get what I want. Where the waste comes in is in sowing them in too large quantities at one time, instead of in succession, not thinning out, etc. It is always worth while to sow all useful vegetables several times over, whether in spring or in summer.

To quote 'Silas Marner': 'There's never a garden in all the parish but what there's endless waste in it for want o' somebody as could use everything up'. And this is true. Even in a small garden, a packet of seed will sometimes produce a hundred more seedlings than are required. With a little trouble someone will be found only too thankful to accept those you do not want, but in the kitchen garden the waste is most to be deplored because good foodstuff is often left to rot on the ground. Always try to give away to those with no vegetable garden anything of which you have a superabundance. Cottage hospitals are very grateful for vegetables and fruit.

One is always being asked: does keeping poultry pay? I know very little about my own poultry, as I cannot make pets of things that have to be killed, and they are entirely managed by my gardener and his wife, who, in their account, say: 'Fowls are very fond of bones or scraps or anything that amuses them. It is very bad for fowls to be dull. When we see a fowl not eating or not looking well, we keep it apart for a day or two, give it a dose of castor oil, and if not soon better, kill and bury it'. I am sure this is a better plan than trying to doctor sick birds. I know no more miserable sight than unhealthy poultry.

But I never keep strict accounts of what things cost me. Nothing one does at home ever pays, unless one looks into it entirely oneself. I only bring the rules of ordinary common sense and proportion to bear on the matter.

May

English and Manchurian Summers; Daffodils;
Summer Days; 'Wood and Garden' by
Gertrude Jekyll; the Common Morel; Homecoming
from Ireland; Phlox divaricata; Double Arabis;
Kew; Canterbury; Longleat; Greensand; Ivy-leaved
Pelargoniums; Begonias; Wild Flowers;
Sweet Rocket indoors; Floating Bouquets in
Munstead Glasses; Horticultural Show; Sundials.

It's Monday, not Saturday or Sunday, so of course it's lovely and fine and I am alone. I wonder why it rains more on Saturday and Sunday than on any other days in the year? Mr (*Maurice*) Baring, writing from Manchuria, said that the Manchurian summer was very like the English summer, except that it did not *always* rain on Saturdays and Sundays.

This month the garden should be full of Daffodils; remember when picking them that the sap of the leaves of all bulbs goes back into the bulbs, so you should never cut many leaves of one plant and they should be left to die down naturally, not tidied away too quickly.

Any bulbs that have flowered in bowls in the house can now be planted outdoors in some out-of-the-way place, as they are not likely to flower well next year, but if the soil suits them they will do well after the first season.

The garden really does look lovely today, full to overflowing and yet nothing flagging. The air is soft and balmy, the first of those precious English summer days which are so rare, but so perfect when we have them, and what I strive for in my garden seems here today. All is beautiful in the garden and the field beyond is golden yellow with soft blue shadows.

To appreciate Miss Jekyll's book 'Wood and Garden' in a way to profit by it, one must read and re-read it.

She says 'The blooming of the Cowslip is the signal for a search for the Morel, one of the best of the edible fungi. It grows in open woods, or where the undergrowth has not yet grown high, and frequently in old parks and pastures, near or under elms. It is quite unlike any other fungus, shaped like a tall egg, with the pointed end upwards, on a short, hollow stalk, and looking something like a sponge. It has a delicate and excellent flavour, and is perfectly wholesome'.

I have, alas, spent nearly all my life, and I have never searched for the Morel! Have you, dear reader?

Any reader inspired to do so should be lucky during the months of April and May. Described by Dr Jaroslav Klan in

'Mushrooms' as 'a saprophytic mushroom, edible and tasty' which 'grows in any habitat with sufficient organic matter in the soil on the edges of well-lit deciduous forests, wastelands and thickets, from the low to the high lands of the whole temperate zone of the northern hemisphere.'

My homecoming from Ireland was welcomed by two new flowers in my garden which gave me great satisfaction and which, if given the cultivation they require, do exceedingly well in our light, sandy Surrey soil. One is a plant praised in gardening books and mentioned in catalogues but which I have hardly ever seen growing in English gardens. I brought my first from Germany. There, it grew in a rock garden in heavy, cold soil, facing north. This is conclusive evidence of its extreme hardiness. It is described in early and late editions of Mr Robinson's 'English Flower Garden' and figured in the second edition under the name *Phlox divaricata*. The Germans add to this the name *canadensis*. But in all the editions, the colour is incorrectly (as far as my flower is concerned) described as 'lilac-purple' which many amateur gardeners would decide with a shudder meant magenta. In

Nicholson's Dictionary of Gardening, a most useful book, the colour is given as 'pale lilac' or 'blue-ish'. This, though nearer the truth, gives no idea of its beauty. The corymb of flowers stands up from a bed of dark leaves on a stalk about a foot high. Its colour is a beautiful real pale china-blue, more like the blue of the half-hardy Cape *Plumbago capensis* than of any other flower I know. When picked, it has the great merit of lasting well in water. I attribute its rare appearance in gardens to two causes, one that it wants dividing and replanting in October in a sunny spot where it is to flower, and the second is that, if left alone, the leaves are eaten during the summer by some unfindable insect. So far as I can ascertain, slugs are its great enemy; they seem very partial to its leaves.

> I 'attribute its rare appearance in gardens' to just one cause – that it has been crossed with *Phlox paniculata*, to produce *Phlox arensii*, described by Graham Stuart Thomas as 'a race of showy dwarf Phloxes'. In these, the pale china-blue described so enticingly by Mrs Earle seems to have disappeared, to be replaced by either white or (again to quote Mr Thomas) 'mauve varieties'.

The other flower is also a favourite with me, and a great horticultural success. We all agree that, as a rule, single flowers are prettier than double, but the *Arabis alpina florepleno* is a very pretty flower. In appearance it resembles a miniature white ten-week Stock. It flowers more or less all through the summer, and though it grows quicker and stronger, perhaps, in good soil, it flowers most freely in poor, dry situations.

Last April, when I was at Kew, the gardener there shook into my pocket-handkerchief a little seed of *Cineraria cruenta*, the type-plant from the Cape, and the origin of all the *Cinerarias* of our greenhouses. It has a very different and much taller growth than the cultivated ones, and I am most anxious to see if it will do in water, which the ordinary ones do not. It varies in shade from pale to deep lilac, rather like a Michaelmas daisy. Getting seeds from abroad of type-plants is very interesting gardening.

(*But*) playing experiments with the sowing of flower-seeds is not entirely without danger. Last year, instead of ordering the handsome, often-grown *Helichrysum bracteatum incurvum*, I thought I would order *H. Gnaphalium*, in spite of the warning *'foetidum'* added to its name in the catalogue. Words fail me to describe how the horrible smell of this plant haunted the garden for at least six weeks. It was like the most evil of he-goats. Once I picked some, and the garden gloves had to be burnt, as they scented the whole hall.

I have had a most successful visit to Canterbury. I stayed with some friends a mile and a half out of the town, which is sunk in a hole by the little river Stour. I wish you could have seen the garden, it was so beautiful; large, flat English lawns, fading away into uncut grass, which again lost itself in a really large thick wood, full of Spring flowers. Further away, and planted between two trees, were patches of Honesty, purple and white. There were also quantities of Bluebells and Scillas of various shades. In fact, for a general effect of 'garden colour' I never saw anything more successful. The season was rather late, but a few fine days had brought everything into leaf, and the whole effect was enchanting.

The tall old trees were alive with hundreds of rooks, but alas! my happiness was spoilt by the farmers having been asked in to shoot the young rooks in their nests. It is a ghastly sport, but it has to be done as they increase so rapidly and are as destructive to crops as the pigeons of old France. The consternation and cawing of the old birds was heart-rending, and going through the woods was not without a danger of its own, reminding me of the story of the French Curé. While taking the air early one morning, as he read his breviary walking in his garden, he felt something drop on his bare head – a present from a passing bird. Instead of being put out, he displayed the grateful humility of his character by saying: *'Merci, O bon Dieu! de la boaté que les vaches ne volent pas.'*

Have you ever seen Longleat? We only saw the woods, and certainly they are the most lovely that can be seen in

England, old, and yet well cared for, and the undergrowth in places composed entirely of Azaleas. We were explained the merits of Greensand, which I have never understood. It lies under the chalk, and comes to the surface in rare places, the glaciers in the ice-age having only occasionally been kind enough to work away the chalk and reveal it. Where this is the case it makes the most perfect soil that can be imagined – never wet, never dry and wonderfully productive. Longleat is planted on one of these favoured spots. Greensand is also to be found in parts of Surrey. I wish we were on it. It is the best soil of all; everything grows in it, it corresponds to the French General's description of the British Infantry – 'Magnificent! Only there is very little of it!'

In the temperate greenhouse at Kew is a new (to me) Ivy-leaved Pelargonium, *Hector Jaconelli* – what a name! – very large and effective, and a pretty, graceful, shrubby Begonia, covered with coral flowers, called *Corbeille de feu*. An *Arctotis* in pots, called *Aureola*, is well-worth growing for those who have a sunny greenhouse, and who like variety. The green-house is much better grouped and arranged than it used to be. The joy of a greenhouse depends so immensely on how it is arranged, I think, and so few gardeners understand this at all; in fact, many of them seem to be colour-blind, or at any rate not at all alive to the fact that some colours entirely kill each other.

One of the sad things of living in a growing neighbourhood is to watch how the wild flowers disappear under the effect of draining, road-clearing, hedge-cutting, etc. This happens not only in the neighbourhood of London, but the same cry comes from round all the large towns: 'How shall we save our wild flowers?' The miniature flora of our commons is a persistent survivor in our dry hot soil. It does not attract the picker or digger, and so is likely always to remain and rejoice the eye of the botanist. But every now and then a favoured spot encourages some plant that grows nowhere else.

When I came here some years ago, such a favoured spot existed in the turn of a shady lane which faced north, and where a slight overflow from a spring oozed through the bank. Here flourished, year by year for several yards, quite a bed of the larger Celandine or Swallow-wort. The spring has now been drained, and the road tidier cuts down the grass each June before the seed ripens, and my pretty Celandines have all but, if not quite, disappeared. I regret it. It is such a graceful little plant, with a foliage as pretty, or prettier than, the Columbine. I tried to grow it, but had no wild place damp enough to make it happy. Its name of *Chelidonium* is derived from a Greek word which signifies a swallow; so says one of my old books. The name refers to a superstition which was formerly generally believed, that young swallows could not see till the old birds had anointed their eyes with the juice of this plant.

I wish very much to encourage the introduction into gardens of the best of our English wild flowers, such as the blue Geranium, the Heaths, the larger Celandine, the wild yellow Toadflax and perhaps above all the Evening Primrose, which is not indigenous; its native country is America but it has, I believe, become a wild plant in parts of England from its habit of sowing itself everywhere. The French popular name for it is *'Belle de nuit'*, a name well-deserved, as I know nothing more lovely than the tall *Oenothera*, Evening Primrose, shining in the twilight of a summer's evening.

> The popular name 'Belle de nuit' is also used in this country for an entirely different plant, *Mirabilis jalapa* – also commonly known as Marvel of Peru and Four o'clock Plant. Graham Stuart Thomas, (in The Modern Florilegium) says 'it should suit commuters who spend only the evenings at home because the fragrant flowers do not open until late afternoon.' It is a tender perennial, often grown as an annual, and not at all inclined to sow itself everywhere.

Have you ever tried the common Rocket, lilac and white, picked and put into a large flat dish, with just a few stones to keep the branches down? It stands up and seems to grow in water as do Forget-me-nots, and looks very cool and pretty in a hall. Of course you must cut the stems long, about two feet. It is a wonderfully beautiful plant if well grown in half-shade, and it will grow in any soil.

I derive great pleasure at all times of the year from a way of arranging flowers of my own invention, which I call floating bouquets. I have the largest size of Green & Nephews' Munstead glass bowl – the one without a stand. This is filled with clear water to the very brim, on which various flowers are floated through the year.

Many flower-heads live thus, whereas, if cut with long stalks, they drop their heads immediately. This is the case with Christmas Roses, and still more so with the later Hellebores, which are such a joy about Easter time; their soft greens and velvety plum colours look so lovely so arranged and picked short, the buds being left on the plant to come out later. These flowers, if picked in the ordinary way, even when the stalk ends are split, fade immediately in water.

If in winter flowers are scarce, a bit of greenhouse fern or autumn leaf may be added, but it is of great importance not to cover the water all over; a corner should be left which reflects light, as in a pond. The flower-fancier may exercise endless inventiveness in this kind of arrangement. Most people, I find, like it. Others think it absolutely ugly.

I went as usual to see the Horticultural Show, which was more hopelessly crowded than ever. I suppose future generations will have large, cool halls for these much prized shows, instead of hot, crowded, airless tents, which are as bad for flowers as for human beings. I did not notice much that was new. I think it such a misfortune that this great show is always at the same time of year.

Some pure white plants of *Verbascum phoeniceum* were very lovely, a *Rubus deliciosus* and a *Hydrangea stella*. Hydrangeas are useful plants for people with small gardens and greenhouses, as they are nearly hardy and so easy to propagate. *Tulipa persica* was new to me. It had several flowers borne on branching stems, inside brilliant yellow, outside golden bronze; also *Tulipa pulchella,* with small glowing crimson flowers. How I do like going back to the type plants! They are so far more interesting, and lovelier too as a rule, than the others.

I have always wished for a sundial in the middle of my grass walks where they widen into a circle. Even in an unpretending (*sic*) modern garden I do not think a sundial is affected – or, at any rate, not very – and I long to write round the top of it my favourite among the old Italian mottoes: 'I only mark the bright hours'.

It is gratifying to find that, six years after this entry, she wrote:

After waiting for years to find a sundial to my taste and suitable for the centre of my green paths, I happened to hear that a man in Kensington sold balusters from the old Kew Bridge, built in 1783 and demolished in 1889. I purchased one of these, on the top of which was placed the face of a sundial, and I have felt it to be an immense improvement to the garden at all times of year. It is sunk into a small, square stone base, and in spring a few yellow Crocuses grow among the grass at its feet. It speaks for itself, and no motto surrounds it.

Mr George Alison published in the *Westminster Gazette*, this charming and, to me, original version of the least morbid feeling about a sundial and dark days:

> Serene he stands among the flowers,
> And only marks life's sunny hours.
> For him, dark days do not exist –
> The brazen-faced old optimist.

June

I came home today from Aldershot. Every now and then one seems to get one's reward for all the toil and trouble and anxiety the garden is. I think I never saw it look so well; it had been held back by the heat and dryness of last week, and the copious rain of Saturday night worked like a miracle. Everything has come out together with the extreme abundance which made one of my friends say my garden always reminded her of Zola's novel, *'La Faute de l'Abbé Mouret'*.

My *Ornithogalum pyramidale* have been a greater success than ever. As I have increased them so I have more to give away. They are a splendid bulb. I do wonder that people won't grow them more. I have said this before, but the wonder goes on, as I never see them anywhere except where I have given them, and they are mentioned only very superficially, with other varieties, in Robinson.

One of the gardening subjects I have oftenest thought out is what I should advise if anyone I cared very much about inherited a large house and a large, ready-made formal garden, with empty beds in winter, and filled in summer with bright-coloured half-hardy plants.

The formal garden, to my mind, is certainly adapted to the formal house, though it often shares its ugliness. In the case of very beautiful old places I think what looks best is either turf right up to the house, especially if the fine timber has been spared, such as yews, cedars, oaks, beeches, mulberries, etc., or if there is a garden round the house it should be in small proportions, paved and planted with Roses, Lavender, Rosemary, Carnations etc. in large masses.

The actual garden for the picking of flowers should be near the house, and yet apart from it. Given space enough, my idea of perfection for those who live in their places all the year round would be to have various gardens, of which some would be at rest and others in full beauty, say, a bulb garden, an Iris garden, a garden for early and late annuals, perennial borders connecting some of these together, a double avenue of Michaelmas daisies, another of Lavender and China roses, and a straight walk or terrace with a formal imitation of the way orange trees are grown in Italy.

We hear much in these days of herbaceous borders, often described in poetical language and supposed to grow all the flowers of the year in the utmost perfection. People say in a light and airy way that the Christmas rose may be picked in the depths of winter, and the Violet flourishes from November till April. All this is really book gardening or newspaper gardening. There is nothing so difficult as keeping the same borders in perfection during eight or nine months of the year. To obtain that result, the herbaceous border can only be the enlargement of the English cottage garden, which needs nothing but loving care, filling up bare spaces with plants grown from seeds or out of pots, watering plants as they come into bud, thinning out vigorously when necessary, mulching in dry weather and covering the bare earth with manure for the winter.

> I think we must assume this last sentence to be heavy sarcasm, occasioned by a failed herbaceous border and the fallibility of 'book' or 'newspaper' gardening – an experience well-known to gardeners.

Some of the best gardeners I know have been disposed to say in these understanding days that the herbaceous border in the old cottage sense is a mistake and not desirable, for a mere mixture, a mass of many kinds of flowers, is not beautiful; there is no repose, no form, no colour even, as one plant is apt to kill another in more senses than one. I think a feeling is growing among the best gardeners that even in moderate-sized gardens certain portions must be more or less devoted to the growth of different plants flowering at different seasons. Everyone must make up their own minds how they will treat herbaceous plants.

I should love to begin garden-making all again, and to my mind, perfection would be a woody slope, with a south and west aspect, protected from the north and west, and with a really good soil. 'What does a really good soil mean?' I am asked. This can easily be judged by the wild flora of the neighbourhood. Woods where Primroses and the blue Hyacinths grow well are not bad; but think of the woods in Somersetshire or near Petersfield, where the wild Orchid flourishes, the Butterfly and Bee Orchids and the white Helleborine, not to mention the more ordinary lilac kinds! The Herb-Paris tribe, with their quaint growth, Solomon's Seal, wild Garlic, Forget-me-not and Violets, all of them grow in these districts and later on they are choked and covered by stronger growing things like Campions, Centaureas and Euphorbias, hiding the Spring carpet of bloom. What a picture this is, compared with the dry commons and miniature flora of Surrey.

> In fairness to Surrey and other counties, perhaps it should be said that these are sweeping statements and not entirely accurate; there are sundry botanical reasons for the incidence of native flora. In any case, Surrey is a large county with variable soil and varying conditions. Mrs Earle concerned herself only with her own immediate area, around Cobham.

Unfortunately, the soil where vegetation flourishes is one apparently less well adapted for the health of man, though if the air is bracing and people healthy, a rich soil will be considered not unwholesome for the future.

I have been singularly unsuccessful with the *Romneya coulteri*, having lost it two or three times over. Humiliating confession! I am now trying it again, and it promises well. The finest I know in this light Surrey soil is growing under a west wall and is slightly shaded to the south by shrubs. It is a very fine specimen, throwing up suckers in all directions, as if it would say 'See how easy I am to grow'. It requires a little protection in winter, with bracken, straw or dry leaves. I killed mine last year by stupidly ordering that ashes should be put round it. Besides its beauty and uncommonness – for one does not often see it – the buds come out in water; a great merit.

I forgot to say last month that the best time to strike a

double and single Gorse, and some of the Ericas, is at the end of May. The little young shoots should be pinched out and planted in sand under a bell glass in the shade. In six months, or the following spring, they can be moved. A double Gorse hedge requires nothing but a little cutting back, and an occasional mulching, if the summer is very dry. When well grown a double Gorse hedge is one of the loveliest and most effective I know, and quite impassable to man or beast. There is one in this neighbourhood that is such a glory in May that even cyclists stop to look at it. I am afraid I cannot say the same of motorists.

One of the June plants which gives me the greatest pleasure, and which I strongly recommend for increase in both small and large gardens is *Dictamnus Fraxinella*. The white variety, *Dictamnus Fraxinella alba*, is much the most beautiful, I think. It is a slow grower, and at one time I despaired of making it do well. Now it is quite satisfactory.

Last June, in a schoolmaster's house in Wiltshire, the whole of a large dinner-table was decorated with this

handsome sweet-scented flower, and the blooms were the finest I had ever seen. As I sat down next my host I thought to myself 'Now I am going to find out the real secret of cultivating the white *Dictamnus*'. His answer to my enquiry was: 'I really don't know. I think it was here when I came twenty years ago. We will ask the gardener tomorrow.' This I accordingly did, and he said it had never been moved. He increased it by sowing the seed directly it was ripe – the seed must be watched or it quickly disappears, either by being eaten by birds, or through falling out, bursting open in the hot July sun; but he said the quicker way of increasing it is by taking off pieces in the Spring without disturbing the parent plant. Both of these methods I tried on my return home, and both answered. The moved pieces looked healthy this year, though they have not flowered, and I have a fine crop of young seedlings. This is one of the many plants worth growing, but with which quick effects are not attained, and patience is required.

I saw, last year, at Wisley, *Tulipa linifolia,* a bright scarlet, and as the catalogues truly say 'magnificent' – but at present it seems to be scarce, for even in the cheaper Dutch catalogues it is marked at 3/- (15p) per bulb, which I consider very expensive.

It is gratifying to note, especially in view of the inflated economy, that *Tulipa linifolia* is currently quoted by Jacques Amand and by van Tubergen at around 10p (2/-) per bulb.

Yesterday I had the great joy of seeing a really good new herbaceous plant – at least, I mean new to me. I have never seen it anywhere before, and I saw it yesterday admirably grown in the front of, but not near, a high wall. The plant itself has flat, large leaves, something like Seakale – and I find it *is* a variety of Seakale. It is called *Crambe cordifolia* – do you know it? It is quite hardy in England, the branching flower stems were four or five feet high, covered with a cloud of small white flowers like a gigantic *Gypsophila*. Long before

I got near it I noticed it at once, as I always do any plant I do not know. It wants room, of course, and watering in dry weather, and plenty of sun.

In a corner of my kitchen garden I keep a space for Solomon's Seals, digging them up for forcing as they are required. Gerard, in his 'Herbal', has a delightful allusion to this plant; he says that Solomon's Seal is good for 'bruises gotten by women's wilfulness in falling against their husband's fists'.

I think all garden-lovers should visit, whenever they can, either at home or abroad, Botanical Gardens or the larger nurserymen's gardens. Glasnevin, near Dublin, is one of the most interesting Botanical Gardens I have ever seen; old and established, and planted in the truest botanical style – viz. picturesquely, and with the earth in parts thrown up into the mounds so essential for giving different aspects to plants. I was told by friends who visited Bruges this year – for, alas! I did not go myself – that when tired of the wonderful art exhibition there, they found the nursery gardens round the town full of attractions and interest.

The most remarkable feature in the methods of foreign nurserymen is the extraordinarily clean and clever way in which things are grown. At Brussels, Linden's Garden has a very good show of Orchids and Congo plants. The Orchids are only watered once a week, owing to Mr Linden's system of saucers, which enables the plants to get their moisture in the nearest possible approach to their natural circumstances. Each pot rests on a little porous stand rising from the centre of a saucer, the space round remaining full of water. There is, of course, no hole in the saucers, which helps to keep the house clean and free from the drip which makes the wood and ground of ordinary hothouses so damp, and helps to harbour all the pests. This description, which was given me by a friend, makes me long for some practical invention that would save the great trouble of the dripping of our own greenhouses in winter. It is most destructive and extravagant.

One need not be in Florence to give one's entire sympathy to the good people there who are trying their utmost to save the beautiful old city from destruction. To destroy old streets to build hotels may defeat its own object, for if Florence becomes less beautiful the demand for hotel rooms may diminish; though honestly I think that, to keep up the influx of strangers, sanitary precautions and a certain content among the people are more necessary still. Five thousand English and other tourists left Florence the week before I arrived, in consequence of a very slight riot. The departure of strangers means ruin to the hotel-keepers and poverty to all those they employ.

When I see protests such as have appeared lately in the columns of our newspapers a feeling of shame always comes over me at the wholesale destruction that has gone on within my memory in our own poor old London, and which few people think about. For instance, the destruction of Temple Bar, because it was thought too expensive to make a road each side of it. Also the clearing away of sixteen or eighteen of Wren's beautiful churches . . . not to speak of the hideous spoiling of the Thames by the railway and other bridges, narrow streets and old houses are constantly pulled down. Only the other day the picturesque almshouses of Westminster ceased to exist. Last, but not least, Wren's work is being disfigured, as most people feel, by the modern decorations in St Paul's.

> Temple Bar was not, in fact, destroyed as Mrs Earle thought, but removed, and is preserved at Theobald's Park in Enfield.

The garden which of all others I most value and admire, and from which I have learnt most of what I know, is that of Mr G. F. Wilson at Wisley. Alas! he died this spring, and one wonders what will become of it, now that the directing spirit has gone.

> One did not have to wonder for very long. After G. F. Wilson's death, the estate was purchased by Sir Thomas Hanbury, and in 1903 was given by him in trust for the perpetual use of The Royal Horticultural Society 'for the purpose of an Experimental Garden and the Encouragement and Improvement of Scientific and Practical Horticulture in all its branches'. The RHS moved to Wisley in 1904 from the Chiswick Gardens which it had occupied for more than eighty years.

I believe it was twenty-five years ago that Mr Wilson first began with about six acres to turn rough ground, part field, part wood, into what is generally called 'a wild garden'. Here I first learnt what could be done by thinning out a wood, digging ponds and throwing up the soil into mounds. The drawback to this type of garden, which I watched with interest, was that it seemed to be a necessity to take in more and more fresh ground, year by year, and now there must be fourteen or sixteen acres under cultivation.

> Five, in fact – still approximately the same as that with which Wilson began his wild garden. The land presented to the RHS by Sir Thomas Hanbury amounted in all to sixty acres. It has now, in 1982, been increased to two-hundred and forty acres.

No one must think that 'wild gardening' is easy, for it depends on endless and intelligent hand-weeding. The plants must be kept clear, or they never flourish. When Mr Wilson made a bed in his wood and filled it with the soil best adapted to the plants he was going to put in, the place was always marked by rough stones from the field. That meant it would be kept perfectly clean till the plant grew strong enough to need no further care. At no time of year can anyone visit the garden without finding flourishing specimens of plants he has probably never seen before. Wild gardening requires much more knowledge than any other kind, and is almost unknown professionally. I have never seen planting well done, from an artist's point of view, when left to even the best firms.

I went with a friend to the great Rose Show at Holland House. As a show it was disappointing, for the season was a late one, and the roses were hardly out, and hung their heads in the intense heat.

The beautiful building and gardens of Holland House remain a unique remnant of the many handsome houses and grounds that used to constitute the suburbs of London. Holland House, in spite of the black smoke-veil cast over it, is still one of the most splendid of the Jacobean dwellings. It was built by the well-known John Thorpe for Sir Walter Cope in 1607. Poor man! He had no son, and it went to his daughter and heiress. She married a smart Cavalier who lost his head in 1649, and Fairfax's soldiers were quartered in his hall.

Even in my youth I can remember the huge 'breakfasts' as they were called (really garden-parties) when many of the celebrities still haunted the place.

The gardens have been much enlarged and improved by the present owners. I was anxious to see the several acres which used to be pasture and have been lately added to the grounds, and I must confess it was with a feeling of astonishment that I saw what can be done with care and cultivation in what is now virtually London itself. The Roses looked as healthy as at Kew, and the Penzance briars and free-growing climbing Roses ramped about as if they really believed they were in the country. The most interesting part of the new garden was an imitation of a Japanese garden. This is a very distinct feature which could easily be adopted where both money and water were plentiful and where the ground slopes gently. It all looked very charming and on the whole this was the best arrangement I have ever seen for growing aquatic plants. The whole of the Holland House garden is a most interesting lesson as to what can be done in poor old London.

After my sister Lizzie married I went a great deal to Little Holland House, the Dower House, which was a glimpse into artistic Bohemia. In those days the artistic set were called 'Passionate Bromptonians' and represented very much the same kind of exclusive circle as that which was afterwards called 'The Souls'. Mr Watts made a most lovely oil sketch of my sister Edith, afterwards Lady Lytton; it was exhibited at the Watts Exhibition after his death. Leighton was very kind to me about my drawing that spring, and gave me a cast of an antique bust of Homer, and allowed me to copy some of his own pencil drawings, and in after years he never failed to ask me to the lovely concerts he gave in his house. Little Holland House was all decorated by Watts's frescoes, and breathed an atmosphere of Italy.

G. F. Watts was a friend of Theresa's mother's, so she had known him since childhood. In 'Memoirs and Memories' she wrote:

I believe it was in the spring of 1848 that Mr G. F. Watts, the great painter, came to Grove Mill. He naturally brought no drawing materials with him, but appears to have been so impressed by the good looks of my mother and sisters that he expressed the wish to draw them, and I remember flying upstairs and bringing him down a sheet of cardboard and some pencils, proud to be able to provide him with something he could use. With these he made two lovely pencil drawings, which my mother left to me, and which are the chief ornaments in my little sitting room to this day. The drawing of my mother shows well the beautiful shape of her head, the face somewhat turned aside, in fact what the French call *profile perdue*. Two little delicate profiles, one laid over the other represent my twin sisters, who were so much alike that few people knew them apart.

> Theresa was always intensely proud of her famously-beautiful mother and sisters, cheerfully accepting that she was 'the plain, plump Miss Villiers' – but a charming compliment paid to her by her uncle, Sir George Cornewall Lewis, redresses the balance . . . 'the twins are very pretty', he said, 'but Theresa is a gain to humanity.' 'Perhaps it flashed across his mind,' wrote Theresa, ever realistic, 'that I was going to be cut out in the family estimation by my pretty younger sisters.'

I was persuaded to go to London, like most of the world, with the idea of seeing the Coronation (*of Edward VII*). The day was foggy, hot and heavy, and the tired-looking crowds were already trapesing through the streets as I drove from Waterloo about midday. The tawdry decorations, the streets and thoroughfares blocked with stands, the side streets shut off by dangerous barriers such as I had never seen before, gave me an ominous feeling of wonder as to what was going to happen. I think London never looks so bad and so depressingly like a mean but gigantic village as on these festive occasions.

> An entirely different view of the coronation decorations was given by HRH the Duke of Windsor, KG in 'A King's Story', Cassell & Co. Ltd., 1951: '. . . very exciting . . . the erection of the great stands in the streets gaily decorated with scarlet bunting and emblems, and the large encampments of troops in the parks registered themselves most vividly upon my mind. However, only three days before the coronation was to take place my grandfather was suddenly seized with an attack of what is now called appendicitis'.

When the news of the King's illness burst on the town like an unexpected blast from some evil genius, the almost magic arrest of all movement produced an affect which, in its own peculiar way, was one of the most remarkable experiences I have ever had. The contrast was so striking between cause and effect. The sickness of one man is, as a rule, so small an event, but in this case multitudes were instantly stupefied by the fact. By the evening the whole world was sympathetically affected by the sorrow and disappointment that had fallen upon London, and the proposed coronation was only celebrated on a few ships at sea, and in the islands of the Hebrides. It was, to many of us, rather a revelation of the methods of conducting weekly newspapers, that though the news of the King's illness was known on Tuesday, several of the weekly papers published loyal paragraphs about the Coronation, including detailed descriptions of facts which had never taken place.

'My grandfather's illness, which remained a matter of grave concern for some days, necessitated a postponement of the Coronation. However, in several weeks' time his health had sufficiently improved for the date to be set for August 9th. This time there was no hitch'. ('A King's Story')

July

If you have a gardener, this is the month when he must be watched and the shears kept away from him; clipping all shrubs into flat banks or round puddings is the delight of most gardeners, or in fact of most men who pretend to do any garden work. This wholesale shearing is quite fatal to all beauty and grace in shrubberies and will ruin many flowering shrubs.

We have had a most unusually hot, dry summer and to go into the garden is absolute pain to me, for all the trouble and labour of the year seem more or less wasted . . . and it is little consolation to know a week's rain will make many plants beautiful again, for the especial beauty of early summer is over. July and August are always trying months here, the soil is so very light and one must pay the penalty; but even the heavy soils, I am told, are suffering much this year. One ought to study with great interest and take note of what survives, and even does better in these very dry years. That handsome, rather coarse-growing *Buphthalmum cordifolium,* now called *Telekia speciosa* – as if one such name were not enough for a stout-growing composite – looked shrivelled and unhappy last month, but it has flowered better than usual, and it is a handsome plant.

My Carnations are much less good than usual this year, but I cannot blame the weather for this. I stupidly followed the advice in some of the gardening papers last year of leaving the layers on the old plants till April. I shall never do so again; here, it does not answer at all.

July is a very busy month in all gardens. The borders must be cleared and replanted, the seeds of perennials have to be gathered and sown, and many other things require attention.

I sow a great many things every year and find them most useful – *Gaillardias, Coreopsis lanceolata,* Snapdragons (*Antirrhinums*). Oh! how useful and beautiful are the tall yellow and tall white Snapdragons! They can be played with in so many ways, potted up in the autumn, grown and flowered in a greenhouse, cut back and planted out in the spring to flower again, admirable to send away, in fact they have end-less merits. The smaller the garden, the more essential are these plants for people who like having flowers to pick; but I warn everyone against those terrible inventions of seedsmen, the Dwarf Antirrhinums; they have all the attributes of a dwarf, and are impish and ugly. The flower is far too large for the stalk and they are, to my mind, entirely without merit.

The ordinary amateur feels the extreme difficulty of grow-ing flower seeds either in boxes or even out of doors, and says that in the end it is decidedly cheaper to buy plants. This is, of course, true of all the strong-growing herbaceous things. But every gardener soon finds that if you want any quantity of one thing, or if the plant is not particularly suited to the soil, it is infinitely better to grow the plants from seed than to buy one or two specimens which constantly die. I would al-ways advise beginners to try sowing seeds in little squares in the seed bed. It is only by this process that they can learn what does well from seed and what does not. I am quite sure no garden will ever look full and varied all the year round without a great number of plants being grown from seed. It is a later stage of gardening, that is all, just as collecting and saving your own seed is a later stage still.

In the old days of bedding-out, lawns used to be cut up into beds and patterns. Now the fashion has changed, and bedding-out has become so generally condemned that most people have levelled and turfed-over the rounds, stars, cres-cents and oblongs that used to enliven their lawns for a short time, at any rate, every autumn. As a result of this reaction, there are now an immense number of large, dull lawns. They are wet in rain, and dry and brown in hot weather. They have their weekly shave with the mowing machine and lie baking in the sunshine. The poor plants, which would flower and do well in the open, are planted at the edges of the shrubberies where, in a light soil at any rate, they are robbed and starved into ugliness and failure by their stronger neigh-bours.

There are several ways of breaking up lawns. One is by turning the lawns into grass paths, along which the machine runs easily, and making all the rest into open, informally shaped beds, planted in every kind of way, bold masses of one thing alone or, at most, in mixtures of two. Another way, and one that finds small favour with gardeners, and with considerable reason because of the trouble in turning the mowing machine round the plants, is to break up the lawn with sunshine-loving specimen plants, Mulberries, Sumachs, Honeysuckles, poles covered with Vines, Clematis, etc. Yet another way is to have a double pergola running all round the lawn in a square, or only down both sides, with a grass path, broad and stately, underneath.

I now come to what is, in my idea, by far the most enchanting plan for breaking up a lawn, which is to sink a small Dutch garden in the middle of it. It should have a red-brick wall all round it, and be oblong or square, as suits the situation. The entrances to it are by brick steps, one in the middle of each of the four sides. The height of the wall is about three feet from the ground on the outside, and five feet on the inside.

93

In the centre there can be a sundial on a square base or, if you have water laid on, a small square or oblong cement tank let into the ground, quite level with the grass, as a fountain and to be handy for watering. This kind of fountain is an enormous improvement I think, to small suburban gardens, and it is prettier oblong than square.

A piece of water, however small, and the sound of water falling from a small fountain or even from a raised tap if the tank is near a wall, is such an added enjoyment to life on a hot summer's day, not to mention the infinite superiority for watering or having water that has been exposed to the sun and air. A tank also serves as a dip for swallows on the wing, and as a breeding place for the beautiful dragon-fly.

Not the least delightful part, in my opinion, of the growing knowledge of gardening, is the appreciative visiting of the gardens of others. On first going into a garden one knows by instinct, as a hound scents the fox, if it is going to be interesting or not. One's eyes are sharp, a joyful glow of satisfaction comes over one on seeing something not by any means necessarily new, but unknown to oneself. But it is rare, in English gardens to find any distinctive planting or originality; I think it must be partly due to idleness and laziness. I can never take up any gardening book without seeing thousands of things I still lack and would like to have.

When looking through old books or modern catalogues, one feels one has nothing in one's garden – but I must confess that visiting other people's gardens very often makes me feel I really have a very fair collection.

A notebook is a most important companion on gardening expeditions. I use metallic paper, to ensure a permanent record, and an ordinary pencil. I write the date and name of the place, then jot down the names of plants and general observations. I have also kept a kind of gardening journal for many years, making notes three or four times in the month, and on the opposite page I keep lists of any plants I buy or bring home from friends, with the date; noting the deaths the following year is instructive.

For those who have not got very good memories for the names of plants, I strongly recommend them, if they can draw, to make a little coloured sketch, however small, on the page of a gardening book next the name of the plant. This would be found a great help to the memory; I began gardening so late in life that I had to get all the help I could.

I have lately been visiting what I call intelligent gardens, and will make a few remarks about them.

In one place where Roses grow well I saw a beautiful specimen of *La Marque* Rose – one of the most satisfactory Roses for a wall. Everyone ought to try and grow it who has room and a fairly good rose soil. The long flowering branches were cut a yard or more in length. At the end of each branch was a beautiful bunch of pure, cream-white roses, seven or eight in number, with buds in between, and pale, healthy green leaves down the stem. Two such branches in a narrow necked vase, bronze or blue or dark green, are an ornament to which nothing can be added for any room, be it in cottage or palace. As a decoration for a large dinner table, nothing can be better than these Roses when they are in their prime – which unfortunately is but for a very short time.

> Mrs Earle has misspelt the Lamarque rose, which can still be found. In 'Climbing Roses, Old and New' Graham Stuart Thomas's entry reads: Lamarque: Marechal 1830. Originally known as 'The Maréchal' having been raised by M.Maréchal and grown as a window plant. Subsequently named in honour of General Lamarque. This, with 'Desprez à fleur jaune', was one of the first yellowish Noisettes raised.

One of the most perfect ways of laying out a long flat piece of ground I have ever seen was in a garden in Salisbury. One long, very long, broad grass path, right down the middle; wide herbaceous borders on each side, with low plants in front and tall ones behind; and at the back of these again, on each side, was the kitchen garden – gooseberries, currant and raspberries, and in between all the usual kitchen-garden vegetables; beyond that was a small cinder-path and then a

wall on either side, shutting off the neighbours. This long garden, stretching from the house eastward and westward, was ended by the river; the tall spires of the cathedral towered behind the house. I have often thought that the same disposition of an oblong piece of ground would turn a depressing laurel-planted suburban garden into a thing of joy and beauty, even without the cathedral towers and the swift, clear, running river.

At last I think I have conquered the difficulties of growing *Romneya Coulteri*, and I think it is now going to succeed. Once it is established I believe it will go all right; but I have tried plant after plant, and they have died the second year, from some mismanagement; one must try again and again. What must gardening have been a hundred years ago when, if you lost a plant, it was so difficult to get another!

At the end of the eighteenth century, amidst wars and revolutions of all kinds, botanists and gardeners and flower painters went quietly on their way. So it has been now, and since I published my second book a great number of excel-

lent gardening books have come out, and as time goes
quickly and fashions alter, I think it may not be uninteresting that I should give a slight sketch of the books I have
thought it worth my while to buy:

In 1900, Miss Gertrude Jekyll brought out her second
book, 'Home and Garden'. Her account of her home is most
charming, and never did bird build a more appropriate nest
– and, as the Italians say, *Ad ogni uccello suo nido e caro* (To
every bird his nest is dear). Like her first volume, this one is
excellently illustrated from photographs taken by herself,
which are very superior to the ordinary run of photographic
illustration. I feel sure that all Miss Jekyll's books will be re-
ferred to again and again, long after the mass of present garden literature is of no more value than autumn leaves.

Next came out with indefatigable energy from her pen
'Wall and Water Gardens'; here the illustrations from photographs begin to fall off and become commonplace. They are
evidently not taken by herself, and have none of the individual charm so noticeable in the earlier books. The letter-
press, on the contrary, is, I think, more useful, original and
instructive than perhaps any of the others. Her advice about
cutting up flat ground by low walls, uncemented and with
earth in between is, I believe, entirely Miss Jekyll's own idea
and is most useful and beautifying. I think anyone who
casually looked at Miss Jekyll's books when they first came
out will be surprised, on going back to them, to find how
much instruction there is in them for all sorts of gardens;
villa gardens, wood gardens, field gardens, terrace gardens
and water gardens. For those about to make a new garden
'Wall and Water Gardens' is most essential. Last year came
'Lilies for English Gardens, a Guide for Amateurs' (Country
Life Library, 1901). Most of these Lily notes appeared in
'The Garden', Miss Jekyll being at that time co-editor of the
paper.

Last of all, this year, comes 'Roses for English Gardens' by
Miss Jekyll and Mr Edward Morley (*correctly Mawley*). I am
much disappointed with the illustrations of this book. I do not

think roses, growing or not, lend themselves to photography, but 'Roses coming over a Wall', facing page 60, is a lovely exception.

Whenever I see in any old book catalogues a work by one of those indefatigable gardeners, Mr and Mrs Loudon, I always buy it. The last one I got is by Mrs Loudon and is called 'A Lady's Country Companion, or How to Enjoy A Country Life Rationally'. It is choke full (*sic*) of information, also full of her bad taste in garden planting, has excellent teaching about bread and biscuit making, cream cheese, etc. Her experience of goats seems to have been narrow, as was natural in the days before railways had drained the milk supply of the country for the big towns, and also before the breed of goats had been improved by foreign blood. We find them gentle, affectionate and highly intelligent animals. But her information is often picturesque as well as enlightening.

I have made no progress in Lily growing the last three years. The Lilies I buy flower and flourish for one year or two, but the summers of late have been hot and unfavourable. In spite of trying every kind of cultivation and receipt, the *Lilium candidum* is generally more or less diseased with me, and the heads of bloom are not really fine. The *Lilium croceum* lasted two or three years, but now most of them have died off. I have one little white Martagon Lily which comes up faithfully year after year. *Lilium Hansoni* was originally brought to me straight from Japan. It flourishes very well and stands re-planting and even dividing. That it has done well in this light soil through these last hot dry summers, flowering every year, should be noted, as I have rarely seen it in other gardens. It blooms in June, and has bright green whorled leaves up its stalk and an orange flower slightly spotted with dark brown. Miss Jekyll says it is a Lily that should be more known and grown. All the other Lilies which were brought me from Japan at the same time some years ago have dwindled and finally disappeared. The late frosts this spring destroyed hundreds of *auratums* at Wisley. I think we may gather from Miss Jekyll's books that a Lily garden means very frequent buying of bulbs. They are certainly more worth the money than other plants, and in a woody dell near a house there is no more delicious effect than large clumps of well-grown Lilies protected from cold winds and late frosts by refined and not too strong growing shrubs and a certain number of overhanging trees. But half-shade and moisture they must have, even if this is only procured by increasing the rainfall from planting them in a dell into which the sides drain.

I left Florence on one of the last days of June with oh! such a sad heart and a feeling that I should never see it again. I am so conscious, as I have said before, of the wisdom of spending the rest of my life at home and foregoing the pleasure of travel, as with my nature, long absences unfortunately diminish the pleasure and interest I take in my own concerns, and regret at what I leave behind comes between me and my happiness when I am away.

This must have been written during one of the spells of despondency natural to a lady recently widowed; she did, of course, see Florence again – and continued to travel abroad frequently.

I do love a night railway journey, because of the chance it gives one of seeing the most wondrously lovely effect of Nature which we so seldom do see – the triumphal march of the coming-on of day. I determined to enjoy it, in spite of the presence of seven Italians, one more than the carriage was intended to hold, who got in at Genoa at four o'clock in the morning and never ceased talking amongst themselves.

It is not only the beauty of the growing light, but the mysterious human awakening, the early smoke that coils from some cottage chimney, the opening window, the man who goes out to his work along the road, every little incident seems to be full both of the poetry and the pathos of life.

In our carriage was a middle-aged couple – I should imagine, brother and sister – and evidently as is so often the case with other couples, the grey mare was the better horse. She travelled with curious deliberation. First, she wrapped up both their hats in beautiful bright Italian silk handkerchiefs to preserve them from dust. Her black hair, I suppose, she thought could be cleaned without expense. She frizzled up her curls and wiped her dark, fat, ugly face. She then produced a huge powder puff and powdered her face well all over. The man bore all this patiently; he was thin and bald and much more refined-looking than she was. He placed a black silk cap on his head. Then she opened a large dog-basket filled with a most dainty luncheon. Sandwiches folded up in a beautifully clean, damp napkin began the meal. Then were eaten large slices of meat and bread, mugs full of rich milk, cheese, and all this with a resigned calm, as if she was performing a sacred duty which she owed, not to herself, but to society. The meal wound up with beautiful ripe apricots, and a home-made plum cake like an English one. The remains, which were carefully packed up, would have fed a carriageful. When they had eaten their fill, superior peppermint lozenges were produced by the lady and shared by her companion; not one, but six or seven were slowly consumed in the same resigned, sad way. Calm sleep then supervened to both, and their labours were over.

I can never pass through this valley of Chamberi, with its beautiful mountains all around, without a strange thrill at the thought that here Rousseau lived and botanised for so many happy years in his youth, or calmly worked in the garden of his early love, Mme. de Warens.

I spent a few days in the neighbourhood of Geneva to see some friends in one of the water-cure establishments so common now on the continent – part hotel, part cure. I must confess I found it rather trying. Illnesses, and especially what for want of a better name are called nerve-illnesses, are, from their very obscurity, quite extraordinarily depressing. Looking out of my window at the gravelled yard and the heavy grove of trees gave me the feeling that I might be in a private lunatic asylum, or even in a prison, though I have never lived in either.

Certainly not. Coincidentally however, she had spent much of her youth in the environs of what was to become a 'part hotel, part cure'. Many years later The Grove, Watford, functioned for a short while as a health farm (see page 22).

August

The Climate of the British Isles; Some thoughts on Gardening; Imaginary houses; Packing flowers for transport; Cottage flower shows; the RHS show; Chelsea Physic Garden; Paxton's Magazine of Botany; Horticultural show in August; Campanula pyramidalis; Hampton Court; Darmstadt; The Extremely tidy hostess.

There is no doubt that the British Isles have a quite wonderful climate for gardening, though it is little suited for sitting out, which many people seem to think is the chief use of a garden.

It is generally believed that it takes six or seven years to make a good garden, but this is a great exaggeration. Much pleasure, and a good deal of beauty, can be got even the first year with annuals and perennials that are easy to grow.

One thing that turns amateur gardening almost into a profession, and with the same beneficial consequences, is that it cannot be postponed. Nothing really does quite as well that is not done just at the right moment. To learn this right moment is one of the chief occupations of the amateur.

Certainly, gardening takes a great deal of time and thought, and so is not particularly suitable for those who live very busy lives or have great responsibilities for the lives of others. But there are a great number of people, young, middle-aged and old, whose lives are not full enough and whose health suffers in consequence. For these, gardening comes as a heaven-sent blessing and a cure for body and mind.

Gardening, to a certain extent, must be done by oneself, or one never gets a real interest in it. I remember, some years ago, taking some seedlings to a neighbour, and I said, 'They must be put in at once'. She replied, 'Oh, I am so sorry, my man is just gone'. I answered, 'Give me a trowel, and I will put them in'. This gave her the idea, and she is now an excellent gardener. It is extraordinary, the objection there still seems to be, especially in the suburbs, against women doing the work in the garden. As an old woman remarked to my friend, when she told her that when she went to live in Hampshire she intended to do her own gardening – 'Well, miss, there is one thing, no one can say there is anything ladylike about *you*'.

But gardening is proverbially the greatest assistance to health of mind and body. It is far healthier and more interesting than spending the summer days sitting in the garden and then ignoring it for the rest of the year. People cannot really love their gardens unless they take some part in producing them. It is not a creative art, like painting and sculpture, but it develops an effort towards perfection.

A great many people seem to me to be afraid of their gardeners. They leave their gardens entirely under the control of the gardener, which results in a very uninteresting sameness, bedding-out plants as a rule being repeated year after year, and he naturally resents any interference from those who know less than he does himself. Some gardeners seem to consider the garden belongs to them and like to plant it entirely in their own way, with very little knowledge of colour or form, or the countries from which the plants come. The solution of both these difficulties seems to me, first to cure your own ignorance, and then to share your knowledge with your gardener; the more you know, the more you gain his respect.

I do not at all agree with the idea that the attitude of an amateur gardener should be a selfish one. I always found, in my early gardening days, that everyone was most delighted to give me anything I wanted. There are a few people who think they ought to keep to themselves any rare specimens they happen to possess, but I think the real gardening spirit is shown by a wish to give away a part of what one values oneself, and so increase the knowledge of variety, both in greenhouse and garden. Everyone should wish his garden and his home to have their own individuality – I quite agree that life in the country would be dull unless we prided ourselves on our own possessions. At the same time, one should bear in mind the old saying 'Be useful where thou livest, that they may both want and wish thy presence still'.

I cannot allow a summer to go by without referring to that dear old classic, Gilbert White's 'History of Selborne'. Even now I do not know why I am so fond of these letters. When I was young my mother gave me the book to read and it bored me considerably. I thought the long speculations about the hibernating of birds – swifts, swallows and others – so tiresome, especially as I knew for sure that they *did* migrate. I, almost a child, knew that.

As I am always planning and planting imaginary gardens, or thinking how I should alter the gardens of my friends, so I am always building imaginary houses.

In the building of houses I think the greatest care and thought are necessary in order to prevent the builders from throwing out the earth of the foundations in a way that produces a flat space in front of the house. Given that the house is on the slope of a hill, or even on the flat, I would rather throw up the earth into a large mound on the north or northeast and plant this with any kind of shrub liked by the owner, than in any way make a terrace in front of the house.

Even in the case of making terraces, they should be laid out *after* the house is built and are far prettier if they slope away from the house than if they give the appearance of the house being in a hole.

Having decided where the foundation earth is to go and how it is to be planted in a manner that will cause the greatest protection with the least exclusion of view, one must try to make up one's mind what one really wants most. I came here to a ready-made villa garden which I knew could never be really beautiful, or picturesque; therefore I decided that what I wanted was to grow the greatest number of plants and flowers for picking and giving away which could be grown healthily in a small space. This can only be done by growing an immense variety of plants, as constant succession is the only method by which I could gain my object. One must always reckon that in certain years whole families of flowers fail altogether, so that, besides the season, one has to provide for wet and dry years.

The beautiful combinations of flower effects which come in all gardens as if by chance come to me also – though sometimes, I confess, by design. But if I were to build my imaginary house it would be on an uncultivated piece of ground – say, wood, common or field – and then I think my object would be to keep the character of the ground as it was. In some ways the flat field would be the most difficult to manage and then an effect of wildness would have to be given by breaking up the ground and making miniature mountains and valleys. In a small space this would be impossible, so that a small cottage garden must be straight in design, a mixture of flowering shrubs and herbaceous plants.

I have made a considerable study of the things that last well in water, as my greenhouse room is very limited, and it has to hold all the plants that are planted out the following summer. In summer the study is for the sake of my friends, as I send away flowers in large quantities, and I know nothing so disappointing as to receive in London a box of flowers, none of which are capable of reviving when put into water.

After a great deal of practice, I really think I have evolved a way of packing cut flowers to send away to friends, hospitals, bazaars, etc., which is both economical and satisfactory. It may be useful to know that Mr Cobbett, High Street, Guildford, Surrey, makes the most splendid long baskets, all sizes, designed by Miss Jekyll – but old boxes from linen-

drapers' shops, or even newspapers answer very well.

The whole secret in summer is to pick the flowers over-night and put them in a pail or foot-bath of water, dry them carefully next morning, and then wrap up each bunch fairly tight in newspaper, hiding the flowers completely to make them air-tight; these bundles are then laid flat in the box, carefully dove-tailed – the tighter they are packed, without actually crushing them, the better they travel. The lid is then put on, the box tied up with string and sent to the station in time for an early train.

Flowers should never be carried to town in a bunch with a bit of paper round the stalks and showing all the blooms. It is very pretty, even pleasant, for the bearer to have a sweet country posy, but very unpractical for the receiver.

This is the month for cottage flower-shows, and much may be learned from visiting them. Always take your notebook and mark down the names of all the plants you admire that are not already in your garden. When you get home, look them up and find out how they are propagated and try to grow them yourself; the same thing applies when visiting other people's gardens. This is quite a different thing from imitating the tiresome amateur who, though absolutely ignorant of gardening, visits the great Spring Show in the Temple Gardens, or some specialist nursery, then goes home to scold his gardener because, among the hundreds of plants he is expected to grow, his specimens of Begonias, or what-ever took the fancy of the grumbler, cannot compete with the specimens shown by the man who gave up his whole time to that one kind of plant. This is one disadvantage of the large flower-shows; another being the fact that the exhibits are so wonderful that the humble amateur is overwhelmed and dis-couraged and leaves the show with a bewildered sense of grandeur and beauty, but no definite lesson learnt. This soon disappears as knowledge increases, and the fortnightly Royal Horticultural Shows in Vincent Square are sources of great instruction to all, even those who are beginners.

I think all amateurs who are keen gardeners ought to belong to this society – partly as an encouragement to it, and also because the subscriber of even one guinea a year gets a great many advantages. He can go to these fortnightly exhibitions, as well as to the great show at the Temple Gardens in May, free, before the public is admitted. He has the run of the Society's library in Victoria Street; he receives free the yearly publications, which are a series of most interesting lectures; and he is annually presented with a certain number of plants. These fortnightly meetings at the Drill Hall are instructive and varied, though they might be much more so. Nevertheless, I think an amateur cannot go to them without learning something, and I am surprised to find how few people take advantage of them.

> Taking Mrs Earle's last point first, the 'few people' of 1896 had increased, in 1981, to an average of 7,622 at the RHS fortnightly meetings. The 'even one guinea a year' has increased too – unfortunately, but hardly surprisingly and the single ticket yearly subscription is now £14, entitling a Member to admittance to these shows, the 'run of the society's library' (now at Vincent Square), admittance to Wisley Garden through the year, and the 'great show' at Chelsea – again, 'free, before the public is admitted'. Members are also entitled to apply for the annual list of surplus seeds, and of course, every month receive their copy of the RHS Journal 'The Garden'.

I was pleased, the other day, to read in the papers that the old Chelsea Physic Garden had been saved from being built over by the London Parochial Charities. The garden was presented by Sir Hans Sloane to the Society of Apothecaries, on condition that fifty new varieties of plants should be grown in it and annually furnished to the Royal Society till the number amounted to two thousand. These gardens and the Botanic Gardens at Oxford are the oldest of the kind in England. The land at Chelsea was acquired by the Apothecaries as far back as 1674. Evelyn visited the Chelsea Gardens in 1685 and mentioned that he saw there a Tulip tree and a Tea shrub. Here, too, it has been said, one of the first attempts was made to supply plants with artificial heat, the greenhouses having been heated by means of embers placed in a hole in the ground. Poor plants! – they must have been rather smoke-dried, I fear. It was here, too, that Philip Miller, the 'prince of gardeners' – so styled by Linnaeus, spent nearly fifty years. He managed the gardens from 1722 to 1771, during which period they attained a great reputation throughout Europe. Miller was author of the admired 'Gardener's Chronicle' (*correctly Gardener's Dictionary*).

In 1834, Joseph Paxton, that intelligent gardener of Chatsworth, started his 'Magazine of Botany', which was finished in 1849. I have the complete set of sixteen volumes. The first volume contains a somewhat fulsome and yet touchingly hearty dedication to his master, the Duke of Devonshire. The title page is quite simple and has nothing on it but the title and the famous Bacon quotation 'God Almighty first planted a garden, and indeed it is the purest of human pleasures . . .' Bacon is delightfully solemn, but one cannot help remembering that Adam found it so very dull till Eve came that he even sacrificed a rib for the sake of a companion.

For the first time in my life I have been to a Horticultural Society show at the Drill Hall in August. The interest centred chiefly in the new hardy water lilies which everyone with small ponds or lakes ought to try and cultivate, I think. But what particularly attracted my attention was an exceedingly good strain of my favourite *Campanula pyramidalis,* exhibited by the Syon House gardener, and flowered under glass. I am quite sure these flowers can never be seen in anything like perfection except grown under glass when the flower is appearing.

One excellent way of arranging flowers in most rooms is to have a table – a kind of altar – especially dedicated to them. This does the flowers or plants much more justice than dotting them about the room. If, however, flowers or branches are arranged in vases in the Japanese style, the more they are isolated in prominent places which show them off, the better.

My principal flower table at Woodlands in the summer, is in a cool hall, away from the sun. In winter I have it in the sitting-room close to a large south window. The sun in summer quickly kills flowers that are cut and in water, but in winter this is not so. On the contrary, it seems to cheer them up and make them open out and look happy.

Never forget, in the arranging of cut flowers, that all shrubby plants and many perennials last much longer in water if the stalks are peeled. The reason is obvious, the thick bark prevents the absorption of enough water. In the case of succulent plants, splitting up the ends of the stalks is often sufficient.

This time last year I went to Hampton Court, and never saw its garden in such great perfection. It was as beautiful as could be, bathed in soft golden sunlight, not foggy or misty as, alas, it so often is from smoke, but with clear pearly distances. The flowers were really gorgeous, and one saw in perfection the modern kinds of bedding. The last of the carpet beds have disappeared. In not one bed could the earth be seen, no pains and no expense having been spared. A lovely arrangement of red and white *Bouvardias* scented the cool moist air, and everything had as much water as it wanted. I have never seen a more successful public garden. I heard afterwards that all this meant a new gardener, and I note it now as an encouragement to those who were depressed by failure in their own gardens, for this year, the weather being unfavourable, the whole thing was utterly different. The herbaceous borders had gone to leaf and many of the beds had failed.

The restoration of the old iron railings near the river, at the end of William and Mary's Garden, is a great public benefit. It appears that this railing had been carted about to various places, some reaching as far as Edinburgh, to save the expense of buying handsome gates for public or Crown property. Its restoration to its old foundation does much credit to Lord Esher's management during his term of office as First Commissioner of Works.

> The 'old iron railings' are most probably panels of the Tijou Screen, a set of twelve wrought-iron panels over ten feet high, designed by Jean Tijou for the Great Fountain Garden, and still to be seen, in excellent repair, at Hampton Court.

(*From Germany*) My hostess and I went to Darmstadt, and enjoyed the trip very much. We went to see not a flower show, but a very unique and, to me, quite a new exhibition of various kinds of gardens; the poor man's garden, the bourgeois garden, the water garden, the colour gardens, one blue, one yellow, one red, different plantings and borderings of flat beds. These were all designed and laid out in the beautiful old grounds belonging to the Grand Duke of Hesse, grandson of Queen Victoria and a most enthusiastic gardener. He handed over his domain to the exhibitors, mostly various nurserymen, in the month of May so that the exhibition could be opened by the middle of August. All the modern fountains and seats, and most of the wood and wall decorations, were hideous beyond words, all in that terrible 'Young Art' style as they call Art Nouveau here, and far worse than our 'greenery-yallery-Grosvenor-Gallery' ever was. There was a magnificent old eighteenth-century Orangery, and oh! such a beautiful fountain of the same date. The circular stone coping was indented inwards in four places, making a flower-shaped design something like the petals of a primrose, the stone just lichen-spotted and grey, sunk into green grass. It was one of the most effective garden fountains I have ever seen. The entrance to all this fairyland, through large wrought-iron gates finer even than those at Hampton Court, was up a long avenue of limes. On each side of the road on the green grass were large round pots filled with blue hydrangeas.

The longer I stay here, the more my hostess excites my admiration. She is most wonderfully tidy. She never leaves anything about in the wrong place for a single moment, and never indulges in any of those terrible glory-holes which are my delight at one moment and my horror at another. I do wish I could be tidier. It is one of my bad defects that I am not.

September

A Homecoming; Dry weather; Pompous drives
to suburban houses; Planting of gardens large and
small; Insects; A Lovely green beetle; The
Encouragement of butterflies; Wild gardening; A
Surrey garden; Pruning; A Suffolk garden;
Treatment of Hydrangeas and Agapanthus; Sedum
spectabile; Figs.

(*1896*) A few days ago I returned home after being abroad and away from my garden for over three months. I left towards the end of May, when all was fresh and green, bursting with bud and life, and full of the promise of the coming summer. In three months all seemed over; the little place looked dried up and miserable, small, ugly, disappointing – in fact, hardly worth possessing at all.

I felt dreadfully depressed, but of course all this was in great measure due to the time of year, the end of August being the very worst month for this garden and one that I have never attempted to struggle with, yielding rather to the difficulties and generally going away. Shall I also confess my own character has something to do with it? Most people say 'Absence makes the heart grow fonder'. This is not my case under any circumstances, and especially not with my little home and garden. The more I live here, the more I tend and cherish it, and the more pains I bestow upon it, the more I love it.

After being away for only a short time I come back with keenest excitement. But when I have been away for some long time, and got interested in other things, I come back in an un-gardening mood, having forgotten all the horticultural names and, if the time of year is unfavourable, I see too clearly nothing but the faults, and have a much too direct answer to Burns's prayer:

> 'O wad some pow'r the giftie gi'e us,
> To see oursel's as others see us'.

I love what I am with, but – with me, alas – *les absents on toujours tort,* and for weeks I have been used to greater beauties and wider interests.

Here the dome of heaven is lower, and no cypresses point upwards. The moral to me is quite clear; gardeners should only go away from home to learn, not to see how beautiful the world is elsewhere without any gardens at all, the science of life being to make the best of what we have to our hand, not to pine for what we have not.

The dryness continues, and we wait in vain for rain. This weather makes us doubly appreciate the small square of cool water just in front of the dining-room window, and the pleasure it seems to bring to bird and insect. Great fat thrushes splash themselves in the shallow edges specially prepared for them with big stones, as they seem much afraid of deep water.

I saw, perched on a hanging branch of the rose growing on the pergola, the most beautiful kingfisher. His blue wings flashed in the sunshine, and, turning his red breast, it glowed like that of a tropical bird. I have never before seen a kingfisher in this dry garden, and I can only account for it, as we

are more than a mile from the river, by something peculiar in the season, and his being attracted in his search of food, by the gold-fish in my little fountain.

An artistic-looking bird table is quite a pretty addition to a garden, and feeding the birds keeps them from getting into the habit of attacking buds and blossoms, which have no food value, but are often pecked at and injured by hungry birds with idle beaks.

Many of the houses built round the neighbourhood of London in the early part of the century were built close to the road, and have a ludicrous and pompous approach of a drive passing the front door with two gates, one for entrance and one for exit. Surely this is a great waste of ground with no proportionate advantages? Most places of this kind would certainly be improved if the two gates were blocked up, the drive done away with, and a straight paved or bricked path made from the door to the road, with a shelter of wood or even of corrugated iron, painted to match the house, and creepers planted along the posts that support it. The space on either side of this path could be planted with low-growing shrubs or in some instances laid with turf.

Everyone who lives at all in the neighbourhood of sub-urban residences must be struck with the extraordinary sameness of the shrubberies which surround these houses and gardens, especially those which are almost invariably planted along the approach. First of all you generally find the road waving and twisting – to give, I suppose, an impression of greater length – edged by a foot or two of grass, ugly in itself and laborious to keep tidy. The shrubs are roughly clipped back, chiefly at the bottom, while as they grow upwards the top branches out of reach are left to over-hang the road. A still uglier way, though more modern, is to keep the shrubs apart by cutting them back in round, pud-ding-shaped knobs. This method has not one redeeming quality, to my mind. Instead of this drive round a grass plot or the circular bed of shrubs, I think most people would find their approach more simple and dignified if that road were straightened, where it is possible.

Now – a word about the original planting. When you take a new house it generally happens that the first wish is to gain privacy by planting out a neighbour or a road. In light soils the common Rhododendron grows nearly as quickly, if planted in peat, as the Laurel or the Portugal Laurel. It is decidedly prettier, and does not suffer in the same way in severe winters from frost.

If, instead of a new house, we buy a place that has been planted for some twenty or thirty years, the amount that has to be thinned out is incredible. People in England are so afraid of thinning out; if they would only try it with greater boldness, they would soon realise how very quickly the gaps are filled up again by the improved strength of the plants.

Where edging is necessary to keep the soil separate from the gravel road, I should advise, instead of the grass, flat pieces of stone, where it is possible to get them, or bricks put in edgeways, or drain-tiles, tiles or flints. There are all sorts of low-growing things which may be planted behind this edge, such as Periwinkles, St John's wort, London Pride and other *Saxifrages, Heuchera, Tiarella cordifolia* and the hybrid *Megaseas.* However many, or few, of these varieties are chosen, each sort must be planted together in groups, never dotted about. Besides the more picturesque effect produced by masses, there is a practical necessity for this; the stronger growing plants crowd out the weaker. Some want replanting or dividing every year, others thrive best when left alone.

What I have said above refers to moderate-sized places, but I think I can especially help people with regard to much smaller gardens, which I have so often seen ruined by coarse-growing shrubs, not one of which should be admitted. If you have room, and can get the special soil, *Azaleas* and other of the smaller American plants are very desirable.

I may mention now that, for a very small garden, no turf is advisable. In gardening, as in many things in life, let your wits improve on what is rather below you. Do not try to copy the Manor House garden, but rather take the cottage garden for a model, improving and beautifying it. Make the background of shrubs take the place of the background of cabbages of the cottager, and have only one paved path down the middle and a narrow earth one round the outside. If you have a little spare space on one side or at the back, then turf that over and plant it with apple trees, spring and autumn bulbs, Columbines for summer, together with Snapdragons and Foxgloves, all of which grow well in grass. The grass must then only be cut once a year, in July.

I observe that, next to pruning and cutting back, there is nothing people are so ignorant about as watering, especially in dry weather. The ordinary, non-gardening mind seems to think that if a thing looks blighted or faded or drooping, it is 'below par' and that water acts as the required tonic; whereas it is often that the dry weather has only hastened the period of rest, and when that is the case nothing is so hopeless as watering anything that is not in full growth.

I visited a Suffolk garden, where I learnt more in an hour than one would do in most places in a week. It was a beautiful, stately, flat garden, and on a very large scale, with tall trees and broad expanses of lawn, which I do immensely admire when sufficiently spacious and with spreading timber feathering the ground. I saw in this garden the finest tubs of Hydrangeas I have ever seen anywhere. They were much raised above the ground, on a half-tub reversed or on bricks, so that the plants which had been left alone for many years, fell all round, covering the tubs almost entirely. The tubs were painted white, and the gardener told me that instead of putting them into any house or shed in winter, he put them under very thick shrubs. Nothing was cut off the Hydrangeas but the faded flowers. By this means they get the damp and cold which only strengthen them in their resting state. In the spring he cuts out the dead wood, mulches and copiously waters them when they begin to grow, and the result was certainly most satisfactory.

The tubs of Cape *Agapanthus* were less fine in foliage than mine are, but they had spike upon spike of bloom, which is really what one wants. He treated these in the same way as described for Hydrangeas, leaving them out all the winter.

Mine were kept in a cool greenhouse, and looked perfectly healthy, but had hardly any flowers at all this year. It's the old story. Everything from the Cape stands many kinds of treatment, but must have a long period of rest in order to flower well.

On the top of a low wall dividing this garden from another portion of it were some flower boxes, well filled with trailing and half-hardy plants, brilliant in colour and easy to water and attend to; the effect was very good, and might be adopted on those dreary little walls that sometimes divide small villa gardens from their neighbours. The evaporation from painted wood is very much less than from flower pots and there is no fear of their being thrown over by a high wind.

In this Suffolk garden all watering was done at four or five in the morning, the gardeners leaving off work at two in the afternoon. This plan, I think, would often work very well both for masters and men during the long hot days. But gardeners seldom like it.

English summers are so seldom dry that gardeners have a prejudice against watering plants growing in the open. Where the garden can be watered sufficiently, watering answers admirably. At Hampton Court in a dry summer relays of men watered day and night and the result was excellent; where it can only be partially done all the attention must be given to what you intend to save, and these must be well soaked. A general sprinkling all over the garden is fatal, it draws the roots to the surface and these get scorched by the sun. Shrubs can be killed by a little watering; at Woodlands a succession of cherry trees on a wall were killed by watering the Violets in the same bed during June and July.

> Mrs Earle seems to be contradicting herself, but perhaps is only demonstrating that *Gardening is not an exact science.*

Now and then quite strange insects appear just once, and then never again. I have heard that it is because eggs of insects are sometimes deposited in baskets or bales bringing goods from hot countries, which, in dry summers, are hatched out in these northern climates.

One summer my *Sedums* were covered with a lovely green beetle. I have never seen him again, but I am too ignorant to know if he were a stranger or only an insect common in our gardens and appearing in some summers and not in others – a usual occurrence with all insects. Sometimes there are a quantity of one kind, they having triumphed over their natural enemies and flourished abundantly. Then for a year or two they disappear entirely. This is an especial characteristic of butterflies.

I thought there might be some way of encouraging butterflies in my garden, where they seem to have become rare, and I asked a friend who has studied natural history all his life whether he could help me to do this. His answer was: "The way to have butterflies is to encourage the food plants of the caterpillars". He added: "Fortunately our three handsomest English butterflies feed on the nettle – the peacock, the smaller tortoiseshell and the red admiral. The purple emperor is too rare for consideration". I, being a gardener before all things, did not think it was at all 'fortunate' that their natural food was nettles. I have spent my whole life in eradicating nettles, so it is perhaps not astonishing if butterflies have become less in my garden.

In spite of all the charming things Mr Robinson says about it, 'wild gardening' is, I am sure, a delusion and a snare. I live near one of the most beautiful so-called wild gardens in England, but it requires endless care, and is always extending in all directions in search of fresh soil. What is possible is to have the appearance of a wild garden in consequence of the most judicious planting, with consummate knowledge and experience of the plants that will do well in the soil if they are just a little assisted at the time of planting.

I saw, the other day, the most lovely Surrey garden I know, though it is without any peculiar natural advantages from the lie of the land – a flat piece of ground on the top of a hill, a copse wood of Spanish Chestnut, Birch, Holly and Fir. Planting had been done with the greatest skill, almost imperceptibly getting more and more cared for and refined as it got nearer the house.

The whole garden was such a beautiful contrast from the usual planning and clearing away of all the natural advantages that generally surround a place which is being built or altered. The land, as a rule, is dug over and made flat and planted in the usual horrible shrubbery style. I have seen such wonderful natural advantages thrown away, a copse laid low to extend a lawn, a lovely spring, which could have been turned into a minature river, made into a circular pond, and twisted gravel paths made round it. I know few things more depressing than an utter want of feeling for nature's ways of playing the artist – as she does at every turn.

I cannot understand anyone walking down a hilly road after rain without admiring the action of the water on its surface, with the beautiful curves and turns and sand islands that nature leaves. It has long been said 'God sends the food, and the Devil sends the cook'. I am sure the same might be said of the owners, the nurserymen and the landscape gardeners who most carefully, as a rule, throw away every single natural advantage of the piece of ground they are laying out, and believe they are 'improving'. What would give me the greatest pleasure would be to have the laying-out of a little place on the side of a hill with a fine view to the south and west, and the land sloping away and gently terraced till it reached the plain at the bottom.

We have had a great many Figs this year, and they have ripened well. No doubt they do better since we have removed suckers and the small autumn figs that never ripen here. It is curious how few people in England realise that, apparently, the fig never flowers, and that what we call the fruit is the flower. Male and female mixed are inside the fig which, when it enlarges, forms the receptacle and encloses numerous one-seeded carpels imbedded in its pulp. This may be seen quite plainly by cutting open a slightly unripe fig. I used to think the flower of the fig was so small that it was invisible!

I have grown to like the large Japanese Stonecrop, *Sedum spectabile*, more and more, because it is a very obliging plant, and will grow even in shade, though the specimens are far finer if grown in good soil and moved into a sunny place in July or August.

I always take this little trouble, and in September I have my reward. Many people will not appreciate the great beauties of this plant because of the colour of the flowers, which are of rather an inartistic magenta pink. But the insects do not find this so, and the reason I grow so much of it is that the bees simply love it. The little, hard-working honey bee, the large handsome bumble bee, flies and beetles of all kinds, and the beautiful common butterflies all flop about it with the keenest enjoyment, the colour of the flower only making a groundwork to their bright hues on a sunny September morning.

October

The beautiful gossamer time has come again. Most mothers now cultivate in their children a love of flowers, but it is astonishing how rarely a love of insects is taught. I do not mean a mawkish fear of killing them, for very often they have to be killed. But I do think that probably the more children understand and admire, the less they would wish wantonly to kill, and at any rate it might do away with so much of the groundless dread and uncontrollable nervous fear of insects which stick to some people through life.

I know some girls who have to leave the room if moths – innocent, soft, downy moths! – come in, attracted to their doom by the cruel lamp. I know others who dare not pick certain flowers for fear of an earwig, which from its silly name they believe to be really a dangerous enemy. Others, again, will injure their health and remain all through the hot summer nights, perhaps in quite a small room, with window and door closed, for fear of the inroad of some winged wanderer of the darkness. All this seems to me so silly, so ignorant, so unnecessary. And if children were early introduced to the wonders of insect life, ants, bees, butterflies, moths etc. I think they would fear them as little as the ordinary house-fly, which is really more objectionable than many of them.

I never cared much for spiders till I heard a most interesting lecture about them, when I longed to know more. The process by which they weave their beautiful webs has only been understood in comparatively recent years. Everyone knows now that the gossamer which covers our commons is spun by spiders. In old days, all sorts of fairy traditions hung about it, as it was quite unlike the web of other spiders. The lecturer said that spiders place themselves with their face to the gentle breeze. This carries the thin thread they have power to eject, with its glutinous end, into the air till it reaches some branch or stone or corner of leaf, to which it adheres instantly. When this happens the spider turns quickly round and pulls, like any British tar, with his two front claws till the fairy rope is tight. Then he fixes it and can travel along it, and that is the first stage in the 'weaving', as the old language puts it, of his beautiful web. Spiders belong to a kingdom ruled by women, and the female eats up the male if she finds him troublesome and unsatisfactory.

My love of Autumn with its recurring beauty does not dull with age or loneliness, and I am often astonished at the interest that is still so keen about all that surrounds me. Perhaps it ought not to be so, for I find quoted in my notebook the following complaint:

> How much is lost when neither heart nor eye
> Rose-winged desire or fabling hope deceives;
> When boyhood with quick throb has ceased to spy
> The dubious apple in the yellow leaves;
> When, rising from the turf where youth reposed,
> We find but deserts in the far-sought shore;
> When the huge book of fairy-land lies closed;
> And those strong brazen clasps will yield no more!

Do you know anything about dew-ponds? They have always been to me thrillingly interesting, and in my ignorance I thought they were just nature playing with us in some mysterious way on the top of the great chalk downs. But it is nothing of the kind. The other day, in a country house, I came across a delightful little book called 'Neolithic Dewponds and Cattleways' by John Hubbard, MD, and George Hubbard, FSA, FRIBA, Longmans, Green & Co. I tried at once to get it, and received the usual depressing answer concerning what one particularly wants – 'out of print', although it was only published this year.

Dew-ponds were originally made by that wonderfully interesting being, pre-historic man, about whom our knowledge has so increased of late years, although our only source of information is what remains of his work. As the book is out of print, I must just copy out the account of how dew-ponds were made:

'There is still in this country at least one wandering

gang of men (analogous to the mediaeval bands of bell-
founders, masons, etc.) who will construct for the modern farmer a pond which, in any situation in a sufficiently dry soil, will always contain water, more in the
heat of summer than during winter rains. This water is
not derived from springs or rainfall, and is speedily lost
if even the smallest rivulet is allowed to flow into the
pond. The gang of dew-pond makers commence opera-
tions by hollowing out the earth for a space far in excess
of the apparent requirements of the proposed pond.
They then thickly cover the whole of the hollow with a
coating of dry straw. The straw in its turn is covered by
a layer of well-chosen, finely puddled clay, and the
super surface of the clay is then closely strewn with
stones. Care has to be taken that the margin of the
straw is effectively protected by clay. The pond will gradually become filled with water, the more rapidly, the
larger it is, even though no rain may fall'.

The technical explanation of how these ponds fill is a little
scientific, but the theory is not complete without it:

'If such a structure is situated on the summit of a down,
during the warmth of a summer day the earth will have
stored a considerable amount of heat, while the pond,
protected from this heat by the non-conductivity of the
straw, is at the same time chilled by the process of
evaporation from the puddled clay. The consequence is
that during the night the moisture of the comparatively
warm air is condensed on the surface of the cold clay.
As the condensation during the night is in excess of the
evaporation during the day, the pond becomes, night
by night, gradually filled. Theoretically, we may
observe that during the day the air being comparatively
charged with moisture, evaporation is necessarily less
than the precipitation during the night. In practice it is
found that the pond will constantly yield a supply of the
purest water'.

(How I should like to have a dew-pond; would not you?)

'The dew-pond will cease to attract the dew if the layer
of straw should get wet, as it then becomes of the same
temperature as the surrounding earth, and ceases to act
as a non-conductor of heat. This, practically, always
occurs if a spring is allowed to flow into the pond, or if
the layer of clay (technically called 'the crust') is
pierced.'

Mr Robert Sydenham, of Tenby Street, Birmingham, pub-
lishes a catalogue of bulbs in which are the clearest possible
instructions of how to cultivate them, both in pots and in the
open, with an interesting account of his own first experiences. If these instructions are carefully followed, I do not
believe the disappointing failures, so often seen when
amateurs try to force bulbs, will occur. He also makes it
quite plain which are the bulbs that should be planted in
poor places and left alone, and those which have to be taken
up, dried and re-planted.

I planted my Roman Hyacinths according to Mr
Sydenham's directions early in October last year, and the
result was more satisfactory than I have ever had before, and
they were in full flower by Christmas. It is a very pretty conceit to plant Hyacinths in shallow earthenware or china pans
with jaddoo, coconut fibre or moss, and place small stones
and charcoal at the bottom, for the roots to cling to as they
grow up. They must be kept very wet. Planted in this way
they look much more decorative in the room than when
grown in pots or glasses. Any fancy or ornamental vase can
be used for the purpose, whether it is flat or not.

The other day I was going round the garden, giving away
plants, when I came to a bed where there were several fine
Echeverias. They had been planted out to grow naturally into
better plants. I offered my friend some, but she said with a
shudder 'What? Those artichoke-looking things? No, thank
you'. I think the dislike of these plants arises very likely from

their having been used too much in those old-fashioned beds arranged in fancy designs as ugly and incongruous as the patterns on a Turkish smoking cap.

These plants are not only kind friends that give little trouble and can be grown in pots and allowed to assume their natural growth, but they are also exceedingly beautiful. I have an *Echeveria metallica crispa* grown to a large plant in a pot. It has been perhaps retarded in its growth by dryness this summer, and is now throwing up a fine pink flower spike. The whole tone of the plant is lovely to a degree, shot with pale purples, grays and pinks, and as full of drawing as the dome of an Italian pine. The thick stem is beautifully marked by the leaves as they have dried up and fallen away. The plant is altogether very picturesque in its quaint growth and admirably adapted for a room or window-sill in late autumn, and reminds one of the corner of a Dutch picture.

The *Echeverias* and *Cotyledons* are closely allied (natural order *Crassulaceae*) and there are many varieties of these plants, all requiring much the same treatment – protection and very little watering in winter, but otherwise next to no care. They can be increased easily by cuttings at any time, starved and re-potted at will, which alters their flowering time. They will grow in china pots, with only a few stones for drainage; or will hang out of Japanese vases, suspended by wires, containing hardly any earth. A large earthenware pan of the ordinary *Echeveria glauca* is a very pretty sight in summer and does well in a north window.

I have been to Mr Barr's today. It is always interesting, and he is so kind, he teaches me a lot. It was Mr Barr who told me last year about making up a hot bed in August and covering it with six or seven inches of light loam; I cannot tell you how miraculous is the result. Every single thing you put into it grows. You can strike every imaginable thing, soft things and hard things and half-hardy things and slips, greenhouse things – everything, in fact, which you may want to increase. It must be kept close and shaded at first. It is simply wonderful, the stock of plants you can get up in this way.

No book I can find in the Gardening Libraries gives a sufficiently detailed account of how a hot-bed should be made, so I hope the following description will enable any amateur to have a successful hot-bed; a labourer could carry out the work, if properly taught.

At least two cartloads of fresh stable manure and dead leaves in about equal quantities is needed for a full-sized double frame. Put it in a heap and turn it every other day for three or four days; moisten it if it is dry. Measure the frame and mark the corners with stakes. Place a layer of the material along the top and bottom and sides of the bed in a direct line with the stakes and then proceed to fill up the interior of the bed, beating it down with a fork. A bed made in January should be four feet high at the back and three feet six inches in front. A good fall from back to front allows the maximum of sun to reach the interior of the frame. As soon as the bed is finished the frame may be placed on the top (which should be six inches deep) and the soil thrown in. The heat is judged by a stick being thrust in and left for half an hour, when its heat will tell you if it is on the increase or decrease. Seeds must not be sown until the bed begins to cool a little. It must be ventilated every day. The heat to be registered by a thermometer is 80°F. in the soil and 70°F. in the atmosphere. Directly the heat begins to lessen from 85°F. it is safe to sow.

Mentioning manure reminds me that the parings and raspings of horses's hoofs, which can be purchased for very little, put into a tub of water and allowed to decompose, make a very excellent and nourishing liquid manure. It should not be applied too strong.

Many kind hints have been given me by various correspondents about the growth of *Hepaticas*. One lady said that small beds with pieces of sandstone were a great help. Another writes 'I was also unsuccessful with *Hepaticas* for many years as long as I grew them on the flat, but when I at last tried them on the shade side of the rockery between the stones, the blue ones have done well, the plants increasing in size year by year and flowering abundantly'.

I found by my letters that a good many people thought when I did not mention some plants that I either had not got them, or did not care for them or did not know them. The last was sometimes the case – but I have, of course, a great many things in the garden, grown in the usual way and doing well, which I did not mention.

The other day, as I was working in my new Alpine garden, a caterpillar fell off a tree just in front of me. His head was round, he had a hairy body, plump and thickset in the middle, covered with moderately abundant hairs; and four square-topped bunches of hair of a pale yellow colour grew on his back. His head and body were green; his long, pointed tail, bright pink. The spaces between the tufts of hair were deep black. His legs and pro-legs were green.

I thought I had got hold of some wonderful rare beast, as I had never before found a caterpillar with a pink tail like a horn. A friend, to whom I refer all my natural history questions, informed me that this was the caterpillar of a moth called the Pale Tussock because of the tussocks upon his body. The moth is pale grey coloured, with various markings, and is fairly common. He feeds often upon Oak, but also on Hazel, Birch and – oddly enough – Hops; he will eat plum and pear.

The pretty maidenhair tree – its Japanese name is Ginkgo – grows well in any strong soil in the south of England. In Northamptonshire I saw it grown like an old pear-tree on a west wall and, as it had been a good deal pruned back, the leaves were large and handsome. They turn such a beautiful, clear yellow in autumn, that it seemed to me a plant to be recommended for wall covering.

Legend has it that the first Ginkgo biloba to be grown in this country was brought from a temple garden in Japan by an early Villiers and planted in the grounds of The Grove. Presumably either Mrs Earle was unaware of this story, had forgotten about it – or simply didn't believe it.

November

Indoor plants; Self-sufficiency; 'Up-to-date Gardening for Amateurs'; Sweet-smelling leaves; Fragrant bags; Forbes Watson on the old-fashioned garden; Greenhouses; Luther Burbank; Cowper; Mrs Loudon's 'Ornamental Greenhouse Plants'; The Garden in winter; Orchids.

(*1896*) I can hardly do better today than tell you about my dark London room, and what I have in it as regards plant life in this, the worst month of the year.

On the end of the piano is a large dish of yellow, green and white Gourds. I grow them because they have that peculiar quality, in common with oranges and autumn leaves, of appearing to give out in Winter the sunlight they have absorbed in the Summer. Their cultivation does not always succeed with me, as they want a better, sunnier place than I can sometimes afford to give them. In a very wet summer they fail altogether. The seeds are sold in mixed packets; we sow them at the end of April, grow them on in heat, and plant them out at quite the end of May. In fact, we treat them exactly as you would vegetable marrows, only we train them over a fence.

On the side ledge of the two large windows I have pots of the common Ivy of our hedges. We dig it up any time in the Spring and put it into pots; before bringing it into the room in Winter, it is trained up on an iron stake or bamboo cane, singly or in bunches, to give variety to its shapes. If kept tolerably clean and watered, this Ivy is practically unkillable, even in London.

Then there are some pots of the long-suffering *Aspidistra*, variegated and dark green. They make pretty pot plants if attended to during the Summer in the country. They should be well thinned out and every injured leaf cut off; tied together towards the middle, kept growing all the Summer in the greenhouse, and encouraged to grow tall. They are then more graceful and satisfactory.

I have two sorts of India rubber plants, *Ficus elastica* and *F. elastica indica;* which last is a little more delicate – it has a smaller leaf and grows in a much more charming way than the other.

Another plant on the window sill, *Plangium liliago variegatum* is of the same family as St Bruno's Lily, that lovely early June flower in our garden. It makes a most excellent pot plant, young or old, for a room at all times of the year. It

has a charming growth, and throws out branches on which young plants grow. It is very easy of cultivation, though not quite hardy, and yet, when grown in a little heat, has all the appearance of the foliage of a delicate stove plant.

In the middle of the room is a *Pandanus veitchii*. This is a delightful Winter pot plant in all its sizes. It does not mind the heat of the fire, but resents frost on the window pane. *Cocos weddeliana* and its varieties are also most useful and well-known drawing-room plants from South Africa. In a brass Indian vase on a corner of the chimney piece there are some long branches of the double plum (*Prunus spinosa flore pleno*). These branches with their bright green, bring Spring into the room more effectively than anything I know.

On a table below the chimney piece is a small flower glass filled with a pretty early greenhouse flower, orange and red, called *Chorozema*, which does well in water. On the table by the side of this glass stands a little saucer with precious, sweet-smelling Geranium leaves. These float on the water, patterning the white surface of the saucer and supporting the delicious scented flowers, so valuable in winter, of the

Chimonanthus fragrans, with its pretty brown and yellow petals growing, as they do, on the bare branches of the shrub.

In separate different sized glasses round the saucer I have a bunch of Neapolitan Violets, some Roman Hyacinths, Ivy-leaved sweet Geraniums and an excessively pretty light red *Amaryllis* from bulbs sent to me this Autumn straight from Mauritius.

On a flower table by the window are glasses with ever-greens. I always cut my *Magnolia grandiflora* with discretion. The clean, shiny, dark green leaves with their beautiful rust-red lining, are so effective in a room.

You know, I daresay, the old nursery secret of growing either wheat or canary seed on wet moss. You fill some shallow pan or small basin with moss, and keep it quite wet. Sow your seed thickly on the moss and put the pan away in a dark cupboard for nine or ten days. When about two inches high, bring it out and put it in a sunny window, turning it round, so as to make it grow straight. Wheat is white at the base with brave little sword blades of green, on which often hangs a drop of clear water. Canary seed is red, like rhubarb, at the bottom, and green at the top. I know nothing more charming to grow in a dull town room or sick room than these two seeds. They come to perfection in about three weeks and last for another five or six. Growing acorns, either suspended by a thin wire in a bottle, or planted in wet moss – five or six of them together – in flat pans, are pretty.

One always wonders what freak of nature makes leaves smell. Mr Burbidge, in his charming lecture, does not tell us, but he notes that the old yellow or brown leaves of the charming Cape *Pelargoniums* are sweeter than the fresh ones. We are apt to pick these off and throw them away; they should be saved, to put into lavender bags with *Verbena*, etc.

On the backs of my armchairs are thin Liberty silk oblong bags, like miniature saddle-bags, filled with dried Lavender, *Verbena* and sweet *Geranium* leaves. This mixture is much more fragrant than the Lavender alone. The visitor who leans back in his chair wonders from where the scent comes.

I think this is a good place to explain the difference, so puzzling to many people, between a *Pelargonium* and a *Geranium*, almost as great a difficulty to the novice in gardening as the old puzzle of what is the distinction between a Vicar and a Rector presents to a layman. In the first place a *Geranium* is really a hardy perennial, sometimes called a Crane's Bill; it is a native of the fields and woods of Europe; the little wild pink one which grows on banks in most parts of England is one of the family, and the best garden kinds are *G. sanguineum*, a dwarf magenta, *G. pratense*, a tall growing kind with purple flowers of a blue shade, *G. Endressi*, *G. nodosum album* (the white form of the wild kind) are all worth growing. All the so-called *Geraniums* which are tender and must be housed during Winter in heat and are natives of places south of the equator, are really *Pelargoniums*. These are of many varieties, those with plain green leaves with a dark mark and self-coloured flowers are called *Zonal;* these can be flowered in pots, planted out during the Summer, or grown in tubs.

Another variety are those with variegated leaves of which the green and white is the prettiest. The ivy-leaved sorts are very free-growing and are more hardy than any other kind.

The most precious of all the varieties are the sweet-scented Cape varieties of which the best of all is Prince of Orange; then comes Lady Scarborough, *Pilosum* which smells of peppermint, *Fragrantissimum*, well-named, the old Oak-leaf, which is sticky and grows into quite a small tree, *Clorinda*, the strongest grower – and there are many others.

What are called 'Show *Pelargoniums*' are blotched with darker colour on the petals and have a different leaf from the *Zonals*. They are not used at all for bedding and are best forced into flower in May if you have a greenhouse.

All *Pelargoniums* can be increased by cuttings out of doors in July, if you have no special place to put them let them rest by their parents.

No one can cultivate a garden as I have done here, and not see the mass of food that can be got out of it. It is not acres one wants, but good cultivation and plenty of labour, and that is just what we can still get in England. People won't believe that all we really need in life is the produce of the soil. A countryman with his allotment can, if he will, keep the wolf from the door, as he can fall back on his crops. But town people must be trained to this life. A town family starve if they are without wages for a week. In fact not only town but country people in England have for several generations been so trained to feed themselves from shops that they have lost the knowledge of how to extract a livelihood out of even the best allotment.

'Up-to-date Gardening for Amateurs' by Henry Vincent, price sixpence, is what I call a most useful, illuminating little book, to be got at 130, North Street, Brighton. In fact the system should be lectured all over the country. Gardening is not Henry Vincent's only employment, but in the summer months he gives it about one-hundred and thirty hours each month, and is evidently a great believer, as I am, in liquid manure. Besides his garden, Mr Vincent puts in eighty hours a week as a waiter at an hotel. Nothing is to be done without work. It is digesting that fact which is the whole difficulty. He does his garden mostly between 4 and 8 a.m. His soil seems bad; light, like mine, and when I first came here I was told by countless people I never could grow numbers of things. Now I know that when we fail it is our own fault, neglecting to do things just at the right time, neglect of making the soil, neglect of watering, neglect of liquid manure, etc.

Mr Forbes Watson, writing in 'Flowers and Gardens' published 1872, was much in advance of the feeling of the day, and is full of what we now think quite the right tone about gardening. In the following quotation he expressed better than I can do it what I want to say:

'Half the charm of the old-fashioned garden lies in that look of happy rest among the plants, each of which seems to say "All plant life is sacred when admitted, my own repose has never been disturbed, and I am confident it never will be". You feel this to be a sort of heaven of plant life, preserved by some hidden charm from the intrusion of noxious weeds. The modern garden, on the contrary, is too apt to assume a look of stir and change; here today, gone tomorrow. The very tidiness of the beds and the neat propriety of the plants contribute to this impression. We feel the omnipresence of a severity which cannot tolerate straggling. None have been admitted but polished gentlemen, who will never break the rules, and we feel that the most cherished offender would be instantly punished.'

I am always being asked about greenhouse plants and how to get variety both for picking or for ornamenting a small greenhouse next a room. It has been rather the fashion of late to say 'Oh, I don't care for greenhouse plants. I only like hardy things'. This, surely, is a mistake. Cowper, that now-neglected poet says:

> Who loves a garden, loves a greenhouse too.
> Unconscious of a less propitious clime,
> There blooms exotic beauty, warm and snug,
> While the winds whistle and the snows descend . . .

I can find nothing in verse or prose that so well describes one's feelings, on entering a well-filled greenhouse next a room on a cold winter's day. It is so true, the plants 'seem to smile on what they need not fear' and one goes back to one's writing or reading refreshed by the warm smell of a greenhouse.

I agree with every word that Cowper says, and his lines suggest what I want specially to urge on those who pass the winter in the country. Greenhouses were new in Cowper's time and the pleasure of them has probably been wiped out – or, at any rate, diminished – by the way people who can afford such luxuries are now always rushing away in search

of sunshine in other climes, and are content to come back in June and find their flourishing herbaceous borders, that have been asleep under manure all winter, surpassing in luxuriance of colour and form the gardens of the South.

One of the least helpful volumes of the large edition of Mrs Loudon's 'Lady's Flower Garden' is the one called 'Ornamental Greenhouse Plants' – so many things she recommends us to grow are now proved to be hardy, and so many others that we now know to be well worth the trouble of cultivation for flowering in the Winter, are omitted altogether. I know no modern book that quite tells one enough how to keep a small conservatory furnished all the year round.

I wonder if you followed my advice and took in the numbers of Mr Robinson's 'Flora and Sylva' as they came out? If not, I do advise you to get now the three volumes. It is really a beautiful book, and the letter-press is excellent; full of useful information. The printing and paper, the black and white illustrations as well as the coloured, are all admirable; so different from the small type, tin-shine paper and bad lithographs which are the usual defects of modern illustrated books.

> Mrs Earle showed great prescience here. The three volumes today fetch in the region of £100.

The man who drew most of the lovely coloured flower pictures (Mr Moon) is now, alas, no more; he died last autumn. There is as much about trees as flowers in the book. Mr Robinson says, speaking of his title 'So I married Flora and Sylva – a pair not far apart in Nature, only in books. The flowers are as the lovely clouds that pass over the Alpine range, the trees as the cliffs and mountains that remain'.

I suppose the public did not sufficiently appreciate this monthly publication to enable it to go on. Perhaps Mr Moon's loss was irreparable. At any rate, to my great regret, it has ceased to be issued. The precious volumes will take rank with some of the most beautiful flower books of the end of the eighteenth century. It is not a book for those who are only beginning gardening, and have all the rudimentary things to learn, but for those who are past that it is full of interesting reading, with special articles by special students of the habits and varieties of certain plants.

In the third volume there is a very interesting article on my pet plants, the sweet-leaved *Pelargoniums,* by Miss White, of the Alexandra College, Dublin. Those that have the prettiest, most showy flowers, have the least scent in the leaves. The three best that I have are 'Unique Aurora', 'Rawlinson's Unique' and one which retains most of the type characteristics called 'Moulton Gem'. It has a hard stem covered with stiff thorns, flowers early and profusely, and is the better for drying off well in the summer sun. Its flower is small and white, with deep crimson spot. As I have a good many plants, and as they all flower at the same time, they make a show for some weeks in my greenhouse, which is much admired. Those which I find do best planted out are 'Unique

Aurora', 'Touchstone', 'Lady Mary Fox', 'Pretty Polly' and 'Lady Plymouth', which has a variegated leaf. As Miss White says, the different versions as to the correct naming of these plants is very confusing.

> It still is. Of those mentioned by Mrs Earle, we know 'Unique Aurora' as 'Aurora Unique', and 'Aurore's Unique'; 'Rawlinson's' is probably 'Rollinson's Unique'; 'Moulton Gem' seems to have been originally *P. echinatum album*, by which name it is now generally known; this is the 'prickly geranium'. 'Touchstone' seems to have been lost to us, 'Lady Mary Fox' is possibly 'Lady Mary'. 'Pretty Polly' is sometimes available and 'Lady Plymouth' is, of course, still a firm favourite.

A reader has asked if I have heard of Luther Burbank. Of course I have heard of him, but I believe he has written nothing himself about his really amazing work. An account of him – man, methods and achievements – was written by E. J. Wickson and published by a San Francisco monthly called 'Sunset'. Mr Wickson says 'Wherever, the round world over, men know flowers and fruits, know of their origin, their development and their creation, there is Luther Burbank recognised as a man of wondrous power. He has done things. Without flourish of trumpets, without asking for fame, Mr Burbank has been quietly at work for years at his home farm near Santa Rosa, California, developing and making fruits and flowers. Patiently, tenderly, enthusiastically, he has worked, with such results that all men who know him give him the highest honour and praise'.

The article gives a very interesting account of the man and his character. He seems to be a better man of business than is usual among optimists. He went, of course, through all the usual trials consequent upon distrust and disapproval. Recognised authorities charged him with holding to fallacies, disbelieving in his researches and experiments; conservatives, in fact, thought that he was making 'a travesty of science for the amazement of the horticultural gallery'. It is always so, and always will be, I suppose; but luckily we are past imprisoning and torturing our Galileos, and true men are ultimately only fortified by opposition, however much sensitive spirits are hurt at the time.

For anyone with a small stove I can thoroughly advise growing some of the more easily cultivated Orchids. For many years all Orchids seemed to me to smell of money, and to represent great expenditure, but this is not the case at all. They only want the treatment suited to them, and the same care and attention required by other plants that are grown in heat. *Cypripediums* come in most usefully at this time of year; they last well in water, and continue to flower at times all through the winter. There are endless varieties of them to be bought, and some of the least expensive are often as good as the costly ones; it is only the new varieties that are dear.

Though all months are equally important at home, one gains but little knowledge in Winter from seeing the gardens of others. One's own garden is never dull in the worst weather because one can always picture what will be, and one can always think over the errors of the past, as useful in gardening as in other things, so long as it is not merely regretting the past, but determining to do better.

December

I have been out for a walk long after dark – or, rather, long after sunset, for the moon was shining bright in the cold indigo sky. At all times of year walking by moonlight gives me exquisite delight. Is it because I have done it so rarely, or because of the great beauty and mystery of it all? I went along our high road, the road along which Nelson travelled to Portsmouth on his way to Trafalgar, never to return. This evening it shone white and dry in the moonlight, and the tall black telegraph poles, which I have always hated for their aggressive size by daylight, in the winter moonlight only seemed to me straight and strong, and as if proud to support that wonderful network of wires which now encompasses the entire globe, annihilating time and making the far and the near as one, ceaselessly carrying those messages of happiness and despair, life and death, which in the space of a moment, in the opening of an envelope, bring sorrow or joy to many a home. Something of the mystery of it all the wires sang to me tonight, with Aeolian sounds different from any I have heard, on this, one of the last evenings of a year that is nearly gone.

We have just been digging up a good-sized oblong piece of ground in the best and sunniest part of the kitchen garden, and moving into it gooseberries and currants, red, white and black. Round this I am going to place, after considerable deliberation and doubt, a high, fine-wire fencing with an opening on one side instead of a gate – which reduces the expense – and the opening can be covered, when necessary, with a net. The reason for not wiring over the top, besides the expense, is that it causes a rather injurious drip in rainy weather and breaks down under the snow. I am also assured by good gardeners that it is unnecessary, and that the wire netting round the sides is a most effectual protection to the bushes, as small birds do not fly downwards into a wire-netted enclosure. My gardener is sceptical on this point, and says our birds are too clever to be kept out by such half-measures. I think we have an undue share of birds.

The trees are now all whitened with a preparation of lime which is distasteful to the birds and insects. After all this I shall indeed be disappointed if my crop of small fruit is not larger this year. However, a late frost may still defeat us altogether.

After some fine, mild weather, it suddenly began to freeze, with hard, cold, moonlight nights. So today I thought of the birds. I now find it prettier and less trouble, instead of hanging the string with coconut and suet from a window or a stiff cross-bar, to arrange it in the following way: I cut a big branch, lopping it more or less, and push it through the hole of a French iron garden table that I happen to have which holds an umbrella in summer. On the other side of the house I stick a similar branch into the ground. On these I hang, Christmas tree fashion, some pieces of suet and a tallow candle (the old 'dip'), a coconut with a hole cut, not at the bottom as I did before, but in the side, large enough for the tomtits to sit on the edge and peck inside, and yet roofed enough to prevent the rain water collecting in it.

On the table below I used to put a basin to hold crumbs and scraps from meals – rice, milk, anything almost, for the other birds who will not eat either the fat or the coconut. But I found this was such a great temptation to the cats and dogs of the establishment, who became most extraordinarily acrobatic in the methods by which they got on to the table, that I had to devise wiring the saucer of a flower pot, and so hanging it on the most extended branch, out of reach of the cleverest of Miss Pussies. If once it freezes very hard, I put out bowls of tepid water. This the birds much appreciate.

This year we are trying the potato onion, which is planted on the shortest day of the year and taken up on the longest. Sutton says in his excellent book 'The Culture of Vegetables and Flowers': 'The potato onion is not much grown in this country, in consequence of the occasional losses of the crop in severe winters'. It requires a rich, deep soil and to be planted in rows twelve inches apart, the bulbs nine inches apart in the rows; it is best to let the bulbs rise to the light, even by the removal of the earth, so as to form a basin round each, taking care, of course, not to lay bare the roots in so doing. When the planted bulbs have put forth a good head of leaves, they form clusters of bulbs around them, and the best growth is made in full daylight, the bulbs setting on and not in the soil.

> From 'The Encyclopaedia of Garden Plants and Flowers'
> '. . . a form of the ordinary onion; it forms a cluster of small, shallot-like bulbils just below the surface of the soil. The bulbs are mildly onion-flavoured and store well. Grow as for onion sets'.

This is a good time for planting Ivies. There are many different kinds, and they will grow in such a satisfactory way in such bad places. In London gardens or back yards Ivy can be made into quite a feature. As William Curtis says in his 'Flora Londinensis' – 'Few people are acquainted with the beauty of Ivy when suffered to run up a stake, and at length to form itself into a standard; the singular complications of its branches and the vivid hue of its leaves give it one of the first places amongst evergreens in a shrubbery'.

This year, fate took us to the North, to Northumberland, the home of my maternal family (*Ravensworth Castle*), from which my mother in her youth, with the whole large family, travelled twice a year on the old North Road to London and back in carriages and coaches.

I was surprised to find that the great changes that have come over our Southern gardens by the re-introducing of the old-fashioned flowers and the old methods of cultivating them are much less noticeable in the North. Apparently changes work slower in the North than around London. I wonder why this is? People there have the same books, the same newspapers and the same climatic advantages as in Scotland, which make the herbaceous plants grow to great perfection and flower much longer than in the South. One would have thought the fashion which has so influenced us would have influenced them. I saw in many places long borders planted with rows of red, violet, white, yellow and purple – vistas of what used to be called ribbon-borders, very un-picturesque at the best, and nearly always unsatisfactory. Why they ever came in, and why they have lasted so long, it is difficult to understand. The gardens of rich and poor, big house and villa, were planted on the same system – perennials in lines, annuals in lines, Mignonette in lines; and where long lines were not possible, the planting was in rows round the shrubberies, which is, I think, the ugliest thing I know. I did not see one garden while I was away whose owners ought to have known better, where things were what I call well-planted. I even saw, in some places this year, what I as a child had remembered as old mixed borders turned into the terrible gardening absurdity, carpet-bedding – the pride, I suppose, of the gardener and the admiration of his friends. This is never to be seen now in Surrey, I think, except in certain beds at Hampton Court; and why it is continued there I find it hard to understand, unless it is that it really does give pleasure to Londoners, and certainly, in its way, it is carried out to great perfection.

I had always heard of the brilliant beauty of Scotch gardens, and the moment I saw them I understood why it was. The seasons are so late that all the summer flowers bloom together. May and June of the South merge into July and August in Scotland, and everything is in flower at once. No wonder the gardens look bright. Besides, the damp air makes the colours more beautiful and the scent stronger.

A great many people use Holly and evergreens at Christmas time to stick about the room in empty vases, round pictures, etc. But they hardly ever take the trouble to peel their stalks and put them in water, though, especially with Holly, this makes all the difference as regards the retaining of its freshness; and if arranged in a glass, not too thickly, it looks more beautiful and does not acquire a dusty, degraded appearance before New Year's day. I cannot bear to see the poor evergreens shrivelling in the hot rooms. We used to have hardly any Holly berries in the garden here, but by judicious pruning in February we now get quantities of a very fine kind.

I have no Mistletoe here, but I presume I might have it if I cultivated it. It no doubt has become so much rarer from being always cleared out of orchards, the pretty pale-fruited parasite being no friend to the apple trees. If one wishes to cultivate the Mistletoe, select a young branch of Willow, Poplar, Thorn or an old Apple or Pear tree, and on the underside slit the bark to insert the seed. The best time to do this is in February. One may merely rub a few seeds on the outside of the bark, but that is not so safe as inserting them actually under the bark. Raising Mistletoe from seed is better than either grafting or budding.

It is so curious, after a full life, to be alone on Christmas Eve. But of course it was my own choice, and not necessary. I could have gone away, but I love these winter afternoons and the long evenings at home. It is also, I think, essential wisdom that the old should learn to live alone without depression, and above all without that far more deadly thing, *ennui*. I have no doubt that training for old age, to avoid being a bore and a burden to others, is as desirable as any other form of education. The changes brought about by circumstances mean, in a sort of way, a new birth, and one has to discover for oneself the best methods of readjustment of the details of one's life. Do we reap as we sow? Very often. Not always. I

am sure that up to now I have never got back in mushrooms what I have spent in spawn. Of course, the fault is mine; I know that.

I often feel that quite the worst part of old age is that it brings us so near to dissolution. I fear everyone will think this is not at all as it should be – and I only feel it sometimes; and perhaps even that won't last.

This is goodbye, dear reader. Collecting these notes has given me pleasure and also cost me trouble. I cannot do better than close them by quoting what were almost the last lines ever written by my kind friend and brother-in-law, Owen Meredith (Lord Lytton):

> My songs flit away on the wing;
> They are fledged with a smile or a sigh;
> And away with the song that I sing
> Flit my joys, and my sorrows, and I. . . .

Despite the dolorous note on which Theresa ended 1898, as she thought, the mood didn't last. And her literary career wasn't over; she was still to write six more books, see the birth of a third grandchild and become a recognised authority on matters horticultural. F. J. Chittenden, Director of Wisley Gardens, wrote of her that 'whilst having no scientific knowledge or training, she had a knack of prescribing a successful treatment for some new plant' – adding that he often consulted her when in a difficulty.

Elegy for a Beloved Aunt

Theresa Earle died at 'Woodlands' in February, 1925, in her eighty-ninth year. A few days later, this appreciation was published in *The Times:*

To friends, as well as to nephews and nieces, she was known as 'Aunt T'. In the 1880s her 'salon' at number 2, Bryanston Square had been almost of the French type. Groups of friends in the artistic, literary and political world met there. She was a perfect hostess. Her rooms glowed with colour, her flowers were supremely well-arranged, and her cooking, carefully ordered by herself, was exquisite.

Her country house in Surrey was a still more congenial setting for her personality. It was here she wrote her books; her writings were very like her letters, eminently characteristic to herself. They are the jottings, not always consecutive, of an original mind, a keen observer, generous and warm-hearted.

'Aunt T' had nothing of the professional woman about her. She was not a student. She was not tied to working hours or business engagements. She had leisure to cultivate her tastes, love her friends, and alternately amuse, exasperate and charm them. She was not always discreet, but nevertheless hearts were bared to her. It was irresistible to have your story listened to with such intense interest as she showed. She was not always accurate or logical, but she was always genuine and free from pose.

But it was not her opinions which made 'Aunt T' the unique factor she was in the lives of so many friends. It was her personality, with its capacity for generous affection and glowing appreciation, combined with a certain shrewd sharpness. Her caustic comments on what one told her, with occasionally deftly delivered digs at the narrator, were a joy at the moment and to look back upon. 'What fun to tell Aunt T' was a constant thought with those who knew her well.

In the years of the Great War she feared greatly that she would not live to the Peace and the return of her soldier son. Some consoler suggested that, in that case, she would know all about it from Heaven. That was no comfort to her, 'No, no', she said; 'no bird's-eye view for me'.

To the very last, her power of affection was as strong as ever, and in her later years her gentle courteous patience was touching to see.

The thought that 'Aunt T' will come no more – 'never, never, never, never', leaves an aching void in the place she used to fill in the lives of many.